SECOND COMING

A Message of Hope from God

Petros Koumasonas

Petros Koumasonas

ISBN: 978-618-85456-1-8
Cover design by Getcovers.com
Translated into English from the original Greek book

The month and year God dictated the books included in this book:

God Forgives and Loves (July 2010)

God and the Universe (January 2011)

God Loves and Gets Angry (March 2011)

God and Money (March 2011)

The Incarnations of God (March 2011)

God and Christ: The True Story of Christ (January 2012)

Contents

I thank my teacher, Joseph Buck Phong, who helped me so God could incarnate in me. I thank God for trusting me to incarnate in me and dictate this book to me.

GOD FORGIVES AND LOVES

God is everywhere. He is within every person, every animal, and every plant. He is in the sky and on earth. This God dictated this book so people would believe, and he could bring paradise to earth.

The paradise He has promised to good people will be nowhere else but here on earth. When paradise comes, everyone will live in it because people, after a certain period of their death, are reborn on earth, remembering nothing from their previous life.

He wants to bring paradise because the earth is in danger from Satan and organized crime. Satan is nothing but sorcerers and witches all over the world.

This book is the Gospel of God because He dictated it Himself. God has never dictated a book and decided to do so by dictating this book, which contains six shorter books.

He is ready to give whatever proof people ask for so that they can believe that this book is from the true God.

Satan tries to deceive people; God, when he decides to write, is not afraid to tell the truth. He wants people to have that in mind when they read this book.

God is forgiveness and love. He doesn't just love the rich or those who have power; he loves the poor and the weak, those who are wronged in various ways, sometimes obvious and sometimes not so obvious.

He wants us to love our fellow man and not abuse our power as a result of our profession or our social or economic status.

Because when we do this, it is as if we are doing it to God himself, who is within every human being. When a person is wronged or oppressed and his rights, dignity, and justice are not respected, then God himself suffers with him.

God's will is that we respect each other. Not to take advantage of our position, our power, or our knowledge to do harm, oppress, or control other people.

This applies to individuals, groups, or states. Who, once in a position of power, use that power to oppress, exploit, or worse, kill, rape, or enslave the souls and bodies of other people.

He wants all nations and all people to be free. He will punish states or groups of people who attempt to restrict the freedom of a country.

His will is that we live in harmony without oppressing each other in obvious ways or in other ways that are not obvious. The non-obvious ways are the sorceries.

Sorceries are the worst thing in God's eyes, and he will fight those who practice sorceries until he extinguishes them. Until those who practice these things realize that they have God himself against them because they seek to control, oppress, and ultimately enslave entire groups of people, even entire nations.

His will is that we respect animals. We can kill an animal to eat it, but not for our pleasure or for easy profit, to abuse animals. Or take their life without first letting them enjoy for a short time this life that God gave them. It is one thing to kill an animal to eat it and another thing to torture it with any excuse.

His will is that we respect the environment and do everything possible to protect it. Respect people, respect animals, and respect the environment. These three must go together, and one depends on the other. We can't respect the environment without respecting animals or the people who are made in the image and likeness of God.

Our strength comes from God. When we do his will, God helps us; otherwise, he cannot help us. His will is to be good and fair with people, but also with animals.

Not to oppress others as soon as we get the chance, and to be good and fair to everyone. Especially the weak, those who have been wronged, and those needing our help. Whether they are children, widows, orphans, or poor people who want decent behavior from other people.

How we must pray

God has made prayer so people can communicate with him. When a person prays, then he communicates with him. Prayer must come from the heart of each person. Prayer must have truth, justice, and balance.

God is on the side of people who are oppressed and suffer, as long as they don't do bad things to other people. Every person who suffers from injustice or oppression, if he prays to God, can receive strength. To cope with the difficulties he faces, and God will punish those who have wronged him.

Our prayer should be on an everyday basis. A few minutes every morning before we set out for our work is sufficient, but it must be sincere with love and fervor towards God. In our very own words, not a prayer someone else has written.

We can talk to God mentally about the issues occupying us and ask for his help. It is better to be on our knees if we can. It is only for a few minutes, and in this way we show our love towards him by humbly and respectfully asking for his help.

We should thank him during our prayer, but also during the day at every opportunity. God will hear our prayer according to our love for him, but also according to our attitude towards other people. He wants us to respect people, especially children, and be good and righteous, just as God is good and righteous.

When we pray, our soul must be clean, and our word must be the word of truth. Then God will hear our prayer and help us. God doesn't want our prayer to be mechanical. He doesn't want prayer to be insincere. He does not want our prayer to be long.

When prayer is long in duration, it loses its power. God wants prayer to be strong so he can help people more.

We can ask for his help when we face injustice from other people, as long as we have justice on our side. And not justice because we are more powerful, more beautiful, or even because we feel closer to God because we go to church or because we pray every day.

He doesn't want people to pray all day, as some people think. But he wants there to be love in prayer, humility, and patience.

God cannot be fooled by any person because if people fool him, they will automatically receive his punishment. God wants us to be good and righteous and not do sorceries. He wants us to have love and faith in him; he wants us to be honest and not wrong any man. He also wants us to have patience with him and with other people. Furthermore, he wants us to have his help if we deserve it.

For a person to deserve God's help, he must have righteousness, love, and balance. He must be baptized and follow his commandments, which are described in this book.

The Ten Commandments were given by Him and are correct. God wrote this book because He has decided to make his Second Coming and wants all people to know his will in more detail, so no one can say that he did not know. From now on, he will punish in a more immediate way those who violate his commandments. He will do the same with those who follow his commandments; their reward will be immediate.

God does not want people to see him as a punisher but as a father trying to protect his children. He also does not want people to see him as strict because he wants to protect his children.

If God did not protect his children, Satan, i.e., the sorcerers and witches, would have enslaved the souls and immaterial bodies of men. He wants people to be free to do whatever they want, as long as they don't restrict the freedom of other people.

When we pray for an injustice done to us, justice must really be on our side. And then, He will give us strength to cope with the difficulties we are facing. But also automatically, without having to ask him, he will punish the person or individuals who have wronged us. No matter how powerful or strong they are, because He truly loves justice and loves those who are righteous.

He will do the same for a state or nation in danger. He will only do this if he sees that we really have justice on our side, and his punishment will be commensurate with the harm they have done or tried to do to us.

When we get help from God, we should never forget to thank him. Each person's relationship with him is a relationship that builds gradually. The more we love him, the more he can love us.

But we cannot love him if we do not respect other people, our children, our employees, our students, our wives, or our husbands. God sees our behavior not only towards him but also towards others. He wants all people to pray to him or to a saint who is united with him so he can help them.

Daily prayer in our home is important, just as important as prayer in church every Sunday or every Sabbath, as it is in other nations.

Our prayer in church with other people and with the priest has a different power. God is glorified and pleased when he sees the faithful praying to him. Prayer in church should not last longer than an hour because people get tired after that time. Nor should it be held too early in the morning so that more people can attend.

His help in the Divine Liturgy is very great. Through the priest, he gives us his body and blood every time we receive Holy Communion. That is why we must receive Communion every time we attend Mass, not just once or twice a year. God feels the love of the faithful and the priest, and he loves them, too.

Our attendance at church has no value for him if it is not accompanied by a good heart, which means having respect for other people and being good and just. He is happy to help people who go to church to pray, as long as they are good and righteous.

God wants priests to marry if they want and have a family. He also wants priests to respect people and people to respect priests. God is righteous and wants the church to be righteous as well, towards the people and also towards the priests. When the church is more just, it will have more power.

God wants all people to be happy. Satan does not want people to be happy. When Satan sees people being happy, he approaches them to take what they have that makes them happy. If they are rich, he blackmails them to take their money. If they are not rich, he makes sorceries to take their health, love, righteousness, and balance.

God wants people not to give in to Satan's blackmail and not to fear him. He wants people to pray to him so that he can help them. He will help people who pray to him and will punish Satan severely.

It is useless to go to church or do good deeds if we are not really fair to all people, whether they work for us or depend on us in any way.

Every man, deep inside, knows when he is right and when he is mistaken. Knows when his injustices can push another person to behave unfairly toward him. And then he can find an excuse to treat him even more harshly and in an even more unfair way.

That is why it is critical to respect and love other people. To be kind and fair in the small and not-so-critical things, but also in the more important things, even if it is not always in our best interest.

God's justice is above all. He loves justice as much as he loves people, and that is why whenever he sees people suffering from injustices, he gets angry and sad and wants to help those people.

But they must ask him through their prayer so that he can help them by giving them strength to cope with difficulties and punishing those who have wronged them.

The injustice done to someone may be obvious or sometimes not obvious, but those who have done the injustice know very well what they have done, and so does God. For this reason, people should not do any kind of unjust act because they will have God's punishment against them.

Those who want to unfairly punish other people with sorceries and make it appear as if this punishment is supposedly by God will have his punishment and will go to hell.

Hell exists and is made by God to punish people who have been terrible people during their lives. He only sends to hell the worst people, those who, in ways obvious or not obvious, i.e., witchcraft, do harm to other people.

Hell, if someone goes there, it is forever. It is not for a few months, years, or centuries; it is forever. There go only those who consciously and repeatedly hurt other people. Without repenting or correcting their behavior and without asking for forgiveness from God and those they have wronged.

If someone wants to ask God to forgive him, he must do so by confession and stop doing injustice to others. And also by doing everything possible to correct the injustice to the person or people who have done it, as well as to their families.

For people who have not done bad things to other people in a conscious and repeated way, or whose sins were not so serious, there is an intermediate state that the Catholic Church calls purgatory.

Purgatory is God's mercy and forgiveness for people who have sinned but do not deserve the punishment of hell. A person can stay in purgatory for a few years, long enough to realize his sins and repent, before he can go to paradise.

Paradise is forever, as is hell. Only good people can go to paradise—those who, during their life, have been good and just to other people. Regardless of the religion they believe in or don't believe in.

God's judgment is about our actions toward other people. Whether we were just and good to other people and whether our behavior respected other people's dignity, life, liberty, and sense of justice.

If, throughout our lives, we have tried to do good, if we have been just and good to other people, then we can go to paradise, be with God, and have everything. Have the blessing, joy, and love of God.

Living this life, we all make mistakes, things we regret and are not so proud of. For this reason, it is important to ask for forgiveness, to pray, and to try every moment to do the will of God. Which is nothing more than to respect other people and be good and righteous with them.

To be good and righteous and respect other people, it does not mean that we should not defend ourselves with all legal means. Suppose another enemy country attacks a country. In that case, people in this country who are attacked have the obligation and right to fight to defend their freedom, ideals, and way of life.

Freedom is the most valuable possession of man. God wants us to be free. For this reason, every time a nation suffers from the deprivation of its freedom, he suffers too.

The Promises of God

God does not want a state to be enslaved by another state or a dictator to restrict the freedom of an entire nation. He wants each country to be free to elect its leader, as in most countries today.

Where the free will of people is restricted, as in countries where there are no free elections, God will not help these dictators unless they change their behavior.

This is God's warning to dictators around the world. But also a promise to people who are currently oppressed and suffering under dictatorships around the world.

A dictatorship is a dictatorship. Regardless of its ideological background or the excuses that the various dictators find each time to oppress their people.

In the same way that he does not want a dictator to oppress his people, in the same way he does not want a father to oppress his children or his wife. Parents should respect their children, and children should respect their parents.

In the same way, teachers should respect children, and children should respect teachers. By our example, we should show children that one child should respect another. Not one child trying to impose himself on another, or one group of children on another.

God is the Alpha and the Omega. He is the one who makes rain, wind, earthquakes, and tornadoes; he makes cold and heat. All nature is under the sovereignty of God. He can decide when to make an earthquake, a flood, or a tornado.

He can decide when to cause a drought or when a valley will provide food for animals and people. Everything depends on God. No matter how much technology has advanced, God will always determine the fate of all countries on earth.

There are times when he decides to punish a country or an entire continent. Not because he is bad or because he doesn't love those people or that continent, but because he wants to help them get back on the right path.

If many people in a country are practicing sorceries in an attempt to dominate other people, then God has no choice but to punish those people. God is ready to forgive these people as long as they repent and stop doing these evil things.

God does not want any group of people to suffer at the hands of another group, nor does he want any group of people to be enslaved to another group of people. God loves justice and will fight all those who do not love justice, do not respect people, want to rule over them, and do whatever they want to them.

He will not allow any group of people to dominate and oppress other groups of people. Nor will he allow leaders to oppress their people, nor will he allow states to keep other countries enslaved.

If a state or nation is oppressed or a group of people suffering prays to God and asks for his help, then God will run to help that group, nation, or state. He has done it many times in the past and will do it in the future. No army, no dictator, and no group of people, no matter how powerful they are, can defeat God.

God wants to show his love for people and his power so people will believe, and God will bring paradise to earth. He will do this through this book that he dictated and also through the many miracles that he will do.

My teacher, Joseph Buck Phong, believed in and loved God. God was incarnate in my teacher without me or any other person knowing it until his death.

God's incarnation in my teacher was a secret. From my teacher's example, I learned to believe and love God more. I owe who I am entirely to my teacher. Without him, I would have accomplished nothing. I would not have had communication with God, nor would God have decided to incarnate in me after my teacher's death.

God protects me and helps me in every step I take. He gives me the courage to write this book, which is his book. For each phrase, he can only be blamed because he is the one who dictates it to me, as he will be the one who will do the miracles. These miracles will be for the glory of God, but also to help people believe that this book is from the true God.

God wants all people to be saved from hell. Hell is the heaviest punishment for people, and it is heavy because it is forever. There, people's souls and immaterial bodies may be overly hot; they may freeze, shiver in fear, or be bitten by dogs or stung by the vultures.

All this without being able to do anything. With no power at all, all they can do is suffer. All this, not for a few years or centuries, but forever. Furthermore, every soul there is isolated, with no contact with any other soul.

The decision to go to hell or paradise is entirely up to us. Every time we decide to harm another person, we take a step towards hell. The good deeds we may do by helping some people do not erase or absolve us from the evil deeds we may have done to other people. To erase our evil deeds, we must truly repent for them, confess them to a priest, and, of course, not repeat them.

Confession is God's mercy. God shows his love for those who truly repent and forgives them. It is the golden opportunity we have while we are in this life, as long as our penance is sincere and we stop the behavior that harms other people. For those who will try to fool God by waiting to repent and confess just before they die, His forgiveness will not be there.

There are habits of people, such as gambling, drinking, and taking drugs, that may be considered sins. But in God's eyes, this behavior is not considered a sin by itself because the person is only hurting himself or herself.

If a person facing such a problem prays to God daily with love and fervor and asks for help with a word of sincerity and a clean soul, God can help him and give him the strength to overcome whatever problem he is facing.

When facing a serious problem, we can, along with our prayer, say "Our Father" mentally three times, and each time add the word "amen" at the end three times. God will help us, give us the strength to overcome the difficulty, and punish the person or individuals who have harmed us.

By saying Our Father three times mentally, God can help us and remove any sorcery or sorceries we may have. Nothing is hidden from God, even if the person who has done us harm is on the other side of the planet and completely unknown to us. God knows it and can punish that person.

The Holy Communion

Holy Communion is a sacrament in which the bread and wine become the body and blood of God. He himself has given the Orthodox and Catholic priests the ability to perform this miracle during the Mass. No man, unless he is a priest, can do this.

God himself said that we, the faithful, should receive Holy Communion in his memory. That means every time we are at Divine Liturgy, we should be able to receive Holy Communion, and not only on exceptional occasions such as Christmas and Easter.

God says that it is not necessary for a believer to have confessed and fasted to receive Holy Communion. He may receive Holy Communion on a weekly basis along with his church service, but fasting and confession may be done once or twice a year.

Another obstacle to the reception of Holy Communion by the faithful, especially in the Orthodox Church, that needs to be eliminated is the practice of all the faithful receiving Holy Communion with the same spoon.

It is a practice that keeps many believers from receiving Holy Communion as often as they can because of a fear of contracting a disease. A small piece of bread, like the communion bread, dipped carefully so as not to drip God's blood onto the floor, can replace the present practice.

The church needs good priests. It doesn't matter if they are married or unmarried; what is important is that they respect God and love and serve him. Serving God means respecting people, respecting children, and being aware that inside every person is God. I am good and kind to everyone and do not abuse my position. I am humble and do not provoke with my way of life.

The marriage

Marriage is something sacred. It is a promise that two people give to each other and to God that they will love and respect each other. He will not go with another sexual partner at the first opportunity given to him. Nor will he abandon his husband or wife for a younger, better-looking, or wealthier partner.

There are cases that force one partner to ask for a divorce, but this should only be done if that person has exhausted every effort to fix his relationship.

For a person to have exhausted every effort, they must have prayed to God and asked for his help. He must have explained to his partner what is bothering him, and he must be right in what he asks of his partner. If a person has done all this without a response from the other person and is forced to ask for a divorce, God will not consider it a sin; otherwise, he cannot help him.

Prayer can be very helpful in resolving the couple's problems. Love and mutual understanding should be essential ingredients in a marriage. We should know that we have a responsibility towards our children. Children prefer to grow up with both parents together because they feel more loved and secure that way. Moreover, God wants both parents to enjoy the growth of their children.

In a marriage, both spouses should try to maintain their love by telling each other many times a day, "I love you," and many times a day, "I'm sorry," even for small things.

When they are angry with each other, they should not say nasty or offensive words on top of their anger. We should not say ugly or insulting words in our anger, with which we might hurt or upset each other.

It is better, when we have calmed down, to explain what has annoyed or hurt us in the other person's behavior or words. Both people should show understanding and a willingness to work through any difficulties that may arise.

Each of us needs to put ourselves in the other person's shoes and ask, "If I were in his place, would I like him to do or say this to me?" This is a rule that we can also apply to our daily lives with other people.

God wants couples to love each other forever. When a couple loves each other forever, then they have His blessing. God wants to give his blessing to couples. Because then they can go to paradise immediately after their death if they have committed no other serious sins in their lives. He wants all people to go straight to paradise and not to purgatory or hell.

Hell is forever; purgatory is not forever, but life there is not easy. People are tested and suffer all the things they have done to other people so that they can realize their sins and repent. In purgatory, people stay a few years, and then they can go to paradise. God wants people not to suffer. He wants them to be happy; he wants them to have his blessing and the joy of God.

He wants the same thing for people living here on earth. He doesn't want them to suffer and be miserable; he wants them to be happy. That is why he made his Second Coming so that he could bring paradise to earth.

The Importance of Virginity

A girl's virginity is important. It is a gift from God. He wanted to find a way for couples to be more loving toward each other. God accomplished this by creating virginity in girls. It is the most precious thing a girl has because it not only helps the couple's mental union but also their physical union. It is a gift that a girl can give to her husband and to herself after marriage.

Each girl should be able to decide for herself on this matter. It is not something that parents should impose. Parents can advise, but not impose their opinion on, their children. God wants to tell the girls that he is not doing them an injustice in this way but is helping them to have a better love life.

God wants men and women to be equal. Equal does not mean the same, but that they both have the same value. Men should respect women, and women should respect men.

God wants all people to have a perfect marriage. For a man to have a perfect marriage, he must marry a girl who is a virgin because otherwise his wife will belong to the man who has taken her virginity.

When a man takes a girl's virginity, a part of her soul and her immaterial body leave the girl's body and go and join that man's body. A man must marry a virgin girl in order for his wife's soul and immaterial body to be united with him.

God wants all men to have the opportunity to marry a virgin girl. He also wants girls to have their immaterial body and soul united to the man they have married in the church.

He does not consider it a sin if a girl loses her virginity before marriage, but each girl should know that this is not in her best interest. A man who has taken her virginity may eventually not marry her, and in that case, it will not be good for her.

Therefore, God advises girls to make love to the man they have married in the church.

Any man who takes a girl's virginity on purpose, to take her energy, will have a severe punishment from God.

When a virgin girl makes love to her husband, her husband will love her more. The same will be true for her. She will love her husband more. When she has sex with her husband, she will feel more pleasure, and the same will be true for him. This is because her soul and immaterial body are united with her husband's body.

God wants to give a gift to people. People did not know how important a girl's virginity is, and that is why they may have married or want to marry a girl who is not a virgin. Nor did the girls know how important their virginity was to themselves and to their marriage. That is why God wants to help couples get back the immaterial body and soul of the girl who has been united with the body of the man who took her virginity.

These couples can achieve this if they both say Our Father together fourteen times for six consecutive Fridays. When they say this prayer, they should be in a standing position and have the icon of St. Joseph and Christ facing them.

They should also say this prayer in a normal voice, not mentally. When both the girl and the man feel that they are more united and love each other more. It will mean that the soul and immaterial body of the girl have left the man who had taken the girl's virginity and have gone into the body of the man she is now married to.

When a couple is united mentally and physically, it helps them not only to love each other more but also to have a more satisfying sexual life together. God will only give this gift to couples who have been married in the church, are both baptized, and are good and righteous.

If a couple says Our Father together for six Fridays and does not feel more united and love each other more, then it will mean that they have committed a serious sin. And they need to repent, confess, and, of course, not repeat the sin they had committed. After their confession, they should repeat Our Father in the same way.

When all the people have read this book and have learned how important a girl's virginity is. Then He will stop giving this gift to people who, while they know, continue to lose their virginity without first being married in the church.

God will forever continue to give this gift to people who remarry in the church because their marriage failed despite their best efforts to save it. God will not help people who divorce to marry a more handsome, younger, or wealthier partner. Nor will he bless their marriage or their sexual life.

Men should respect girls and their virginity. To a girl, it's the most precious thing she has. They should see girls as they see their sister or their mother. They shouldn't take a girl's virginity. Every man should take only the virginity of the woman he has married in the church.

A man and a woman, if they want to have a happy marriage, should not marry out of self-interest but because they truly love each other. They should not marry someone just because he is handsome or she is beautiful but because they truly love each other. They should not marry just because one tells the other that they love them, but because they really love each other.

When a man truly loves a girl, he will be faithful to her for the rest of his life. He will love her in good times and bad. He will love her even when she is old; he will love her even when she is sick; he will love her even when she is dying; he will love her forever. The same will be true for a girl.

The ideal sex

Sexuality is a gift from God, and people have the right to and should enjoy it. God does not allow adultery, but people have the right to be sexually happy with their partner they have married in the church.

God wants to bring paradise to earth. Paradise without a happy and rich sexual life cannot exist. That is why he decided to talk about this issue.

He wanted to write about this subject later in another book, but finally, he decided to talk about this crucial and, at the same time, very sensitive issue in this book.

God has made man and knows every detail about the human body. He knows that in order for a man to be happy, it is not only enough for him to have material goods, but he must also have a happy and rich sexual life.

Perfect sex is an essential ingredient of paradise. It presupposes orgasm with the sexual organs and anus. Perfect sex gives joy to people and helps them have good health and longevity. The anus is a point that can provide pleasure to both men and women who are not homosexual but want to have a richer sex life between them.

God does not consider it a sin, nor is a man a homosexual who, while having sex with his wife, also has anal pleasure. The same is true of a woman who has sex with her husband.

When a man has an orgasm with his sexual organs and anus, he is happier and kinder not only to other people but also to the animals. An anal orgasm gives joy to the whole body and to the soul.

The anus is a point that, while it can give pleasure, is also a very sensitive point, and therefore should never be done without the will of both spouses. God has made man and knows that he can have an orgasm with the sexual organs and anus.

Oral sex between a man and his wife is not considered a sin by God. A woman can give pleasure to her husband in this way, and so can a man to his wife. A man's semen, if swallowed by his wife, helps her to love her husband more, but it also helps the husband to love his wife more.

God wants to give people a gift. That gift is the ability to have a perfect orgasm. A perfect orgasm presupposes perfect sex. Perfect sex can only be achieved with God's help. If a person wants to have perfect sex, he or she must pray to God and ask for His help. God will only help people who do not wrong or oppress other people.

Perfect sex presupposes love with a person we have married in church. God wants couples to marry in the church so that He can help them. When a couple gets married in the church, God blesses not only their marriage but also their sexual life.

Another secret to a perfect sex life is massage. Massage can be done by both partners and can involve all parts of the body. Another secret is kissing, which can involve all parts of the body.

Another secret is to say whatever we want to our partner during the sexual act, except for words or phrases that may be offensive to our partner.

Another secret is to imagine another sexual partner if we want to during the sexual act. God wants people to feel that they are not lacking anything.

Another secret to a happy and rich sex life is for the husband to do to his wife whatever she asks in bed and for the wife to do the same to her husband. Love and mutual understanding must prevail during the sexual act.

God decided to reveal these erotic secrets to people so that they could enjoy love and life in general more. He will punish any person who accuses the person writing this book with his dictation. He wants to bring paradise to earth, and paradise without a happy and rich love life cannot exist.

This does not mean that God allows adultery or the sexual exploitation of people. But on the other side, he wants people to enjoy love without thinking they are doing something wrong.

God wants to tell the church that they should not reject this book because God has told people the truth about sexuality. He never said that people should not enjoy love-making. What He said was, "Thou shalt not commit adultery." God does not love adultery, and it is a sin.

God does not want people to give up their husband or wife once they find a better-looking, younger, or richer partner. He wants people to feel secure in their marriage. The wife is to be faithful to her husband, just as he should be faithful to her.

He does not want people to divorce. If a woman is having problems with her partner, she should try to explain to him what behaviors are making her unhappy in her marriage, as has been mentioned before. She should also pray to God and ask for his help.

If all this fails, then she can ask her partner for a divorce. God does not want a person to be unhappy in their marriage, but He also does not want couples to divorce at the first sign of trouble. He wants divorce to be the last, not the easy, solution.

Masturbation is not a sin and can be an outlet, especially for young people, men and women, until marriage. The hormonal system needs a good sexual life. When a person is not married, he or she can have a good sex life by masturbating. God wants all people to have a good sexual life. That is why he talks about masturbation.

Abortion is a sin, and a couple should never resort to it. If a couple does not want to have children, they should take the necessary precautions. It is not a sin to take precautions if one would rather not have children.

If a mother cannot raise her child, it is better to give it to another family to raise it or to an institution than to have an abortion. The only time God does not consider abortion a sin is in cases of serious health problems in the fetus.

He has a special love for orphaned children, widows, and women who raise their children alone. Whoever wrongs a widowed woman or an orphaned child will receive double punishment from God.

The Baptism

When a child is born, it should be baptized as soon as possible. If that is possible within the first fifteen days of his life, to protect it from dangers that the parents do not know about. Baptism is best to be done without water in order not to frighten the child. And because God wants baptism not to be an unpleasant experience for the child, He wants it to be a pleasant experience. If the priest wants, he can form the shape of the cross on the child's forehead with a little water.

God does not necessarily need water to bless a child, nor is a second baptism necessary when the child is older. What God does once, he does not need to repeat it.

He also needs the love of the priest and parents and a prayer that lasts no more than fifteen minutes. Children get tired and scared when priests put them in water, so he wants the prayer to be short and without the water.

Satan wants all people to be atheists. Satan wants all people to be godless so he can more easily hurt them. God wants all people to believe in Him and pray to Him so He can help them.

Wants to help people. That is why he wrote this book. This book is the wisdom and truth of God. No man can promise what he promises in this book.

He wants all people to live with dignity, respect, and justice. Wants all people to live a happy life. He wants all nations and all people to be free. He will punish states or groups of individuals who attempt to restrict the freedom of a nation.

People who accumulate money by wronging and oppressing other people will not enjoy their money. They're going to get his punishment. He will not let them continue to oppress and wrong other people.

He wants justice. Will do everything for those who are wronged and oppressed, whether in visible or non-visible ways. The non-visible ways, i.e., sorceries, are often more dangerous, so God will destroy those who wrong and oppress other people with sorceries. They will pay in this life and in the next. They will have a reserved place in hell unless they repent, ask for forgiveness and mercy, and stop making sorceries. God knows them all.

This book is the final warning to all those who oppress and wrong other people with witchcraft. God has decided to make his Second Coming and bring the paradise he has promised to people.

Good people should not be afraid; only those who oppress and wrong other people should be afraid and repent. If they do not repent, their punishment will be immediate and harsh.

Good people should rejoice in God's decision to bring paradise to earth. Which means slowly hunger, poverty, wars, injustice, oppression, witchcraft, and natural disasters will cease.

God will perform many miracles to show his power and his love for people. He wants people to believe in this book so that he can bring paradise to earth.

God and the Universe

God created the universe in six days. These six days were not consecutive, but there were some years between one day and the next for Him to prepare what he would create.

On the first day, he created the great explosion, the Big Bang; on the second day, he created the planets and the entire universe. The third day created the oceans, and the fourth day created the plants. On the fifth day, God created the birds, poultry, animals, and fish, and on the sixth day, he created man.

Scientists are right when they say that the world was created by the Big Bang. But the Big Bang was created by

God, as were the exact dimensions of the universe, so it can overcome the law of gravity.

The age of the universe is about nine billion years. The age of all human beings is the same as the age of the universe.

Man is immortal; only his physical body dies, and after ten to fifteen years, he is reborn to live a new life here on earth.

If a man goes to purgatory, he will be reborn after twenty to twenty-five years on earth. Every man is always born with the same sex. If he is a man, he is always born as a man, and if she is a woman, she is always born as a woman.

Immediately after the creation of the universe, God made the laws by which the entire universe is governed, which are justice, love, and balance.

These laws are important, and no human being can be exempt from them. God, through this book, also gives the interpretation of these laws.

Satan, i.e., witches and sorcerers, believes that they can outsmart God and that with their sorceries they can circumvent these laws, but this is not true. No man, no matter how many sorceries he does, can circumvent or nullify the laws of God.

He created man from nothing, and so did the stars, the galaxies, and the entire universe. Before that, there was the total darkness. God created all of this out of love for creation.

God created the universe in the same way he created man. Man has a brain, and the universe has a brain. The brain of the universe is God. God is one for the entire universe.

The different organs of the body correspond to the different cosmos or universes that exist in the entire universe. The black holes that exist in the universe are nine, as many as the holes the human body has.

The planets that have life and are inhabited by people in the same form as ours are three, as many as the basic functions of the human body. The basic functions of the human body are the kidneys, the heart, and the liver.

Earth corresponds to the kidneys, and the other two planets correspond to the other two organs of the body. The planets that have life are found in the three different cosmos, or universes, that exist in the entire universe. In each universe, there is only one planet that has life.

In order for the universe to function properly and in harmony, the everyday life of the people on these three planets must also function properly. If the life of the people on one planet is degraded, then the entire universe suffers. Because the universe functions like a human organism, where one organ affects the other.

People's lives can be degraded on a planet if Satan prevails. That is why God will never let Satan, i.e., sorcerers and witches, prevail on earth.

Satan has not prevailed on the other two planets. The people there, with God's help, have managed to have justice, love, and balance. That is, they have managed to have paradise.

Now it is the turn of the earth, with God's help, to succeed in acquiring justice, love, and balance. When the earth succeeds in having justice, love, and balance, then it will have paradise.

Paradise on earth is not something distant. It can come within a few years. God will give all the knowledge that He has given to the other two planets, which are inhabited by people who have the same form as ours. There the people do not wrong, do not oppress, and do not make sorceries.

They have security with God's help; they have a perfect climate, enough food and water, and a clean environment; they have the shell with which they can fly and go to any part of their planet they want; they have the three containers with the basic food items that God fills when they are empty; they have the device that gives them free electricity by the power of gravity; they have perfect health; they can live to be a hundred and fifty years old; they have a perfect sexual life; they have it all.

God wants to do the same on earth. He wishes to give all of that to people on earth. He has promised paradise to people, and now the time has come to fulfill his promise and bring paradise to earth.

His work is to bring paradise to all three planets inhabited by humans. Now it is the turn of the earth to have paradise.

The entire universe is a perfect system. For the universe to function properly, all three planets must function properly. God wants the entire universe to work in harmony. He wants the entire universe to work in harmony because He is harmony. He doesn't want disharmony; he wants harmony. Wants justice, love, and balance.

People who die go to paradise. Paradise is nothing more than their return to earth to live another life, remembering nothing of their previous life. That is why, no matter how hard people search, they will find nothing about their previous life. If someone promises them that they can help them find something about their past life, it will be a lie to take advantage of them.

Those who go to purgatory will also be able to go to paradise after a certain period of twenty to twenty-five years. Which means they will be able to return to Earth and have the opportunity to live a new life.

God sends people who have died to the countries where they lived before they died. He does this to make the environment more familiar to the children who are born and to make them feel more comfortable. Only in exceptional cases and if there is a good reason, he may send a person to a country apart from the one he lived in before to help him.

Since the beginning of the creation of the world, God has made a certain number of souls dwell on earth. Therefore, people should not worry about the population on earth increasing too much. The number of souls God has made is nine billion. He is literally the Father of all human beings because He has created them.

God wants all people to have the opportunity to live a new life, remembering nothing from their previous life.

He has promised paradise to people, and that is why he has now decided to reign on earth and bring the paradise to earth. Only those who go to hell will not have the chance to be born again. They will stay in hell forever.

If a person faces difficulties in his life, he is not entitled to end his life on his own to start a new life. Our life is from God, and we should never end it on our own.

Only if a person is seriously ill and is kept alive by mechanical means. That person, or his relatives, if he cannot do so himself, is entitled to ask to remove the artificial means that are keeping him alive.

The Saints

Saints, too, are not born again but are close to God to help him in his work. Such real saints are not many. They are Christ, Pope John Paul II, the teacher of the person writing this book, Joseph Buck Phong, and the Holy Mary. These saints are united with Him and can give help to people if they pray to them.

Many times, people pray to a saint who is not really a saint, and they get help. This is because God sees their faith and helps them, not the specific saint they pray to.

If a saint wants to, he can resign from his position and be reborn on earth as a mere human being, but no saint wants to do that. God has given all men free will, and the same is true for the saints. He does not want any man to feel oppressed because, when a man is oppressed, then God is also oppressed.

The saints are united with God, and only He can decide which people will be united with him. The church believes she can make a man a saint. But this is not true.

God decides to make saints only people who have helped him, as were Jesus and Holy Mary.

Pope John Paul II also helped God because, during his time as pope, he always listened to what He advised him to do, and he did it immediately.

St. Joseph Buck Phong helped God very much. God was incarnated in St. Joseph Buck Phong before his incarnation in Petros, and he always did God's will until the last moment of his life.

God usually decides right after a person's death whether to make him a saint or not. Because He knows every detail of each person's life. He will also make other people saints who have helped him or will help him in the future.

The basic laws of the universe

God created man in His own image and likeness and gave him the ability to create, to distinguish good from evil and right from wrong, to have emotions, to have drives, and to be able to reproduce.

He gave him an environment that could provide him with all the things he needed to survive. Gave him free will; gave him the ability to have freedom of thought but also freedom of action.

On the other hand, He made laws that, if man violates them, he will suffer the consequences. These laws are simple: justice, love, and balance. If one of these is missing, then we are doing something wrong; if two of them are missing, then we are in big trouble; and if all three are missing, then we are with Satan.

Satan exists, and he is nothing more than people who do sorceries. They do these sorceries with the assistance of other sorcerers who have died. These sorcerers who have died are nothing more than the demons. The purpose of Satan, i.e., the sorcerers, is to prevail on earth and to enslave the souls and bodies of men. God has allowed this until now, but from now on, He will not allow it.

God decided to make His Second Coming because He saw Satan was an actual threat to people. He has already enslaved many people and threatens to enslave the whole earth. God will fight Satan. All the sorcerers who have died will go to hell, and so will those who die from now on if they do not repent. God will not allow them to be among the rest of the people.

The sorcerers and witches will no longer have the help of demons to do their sorceries. Nor will the demons be able to enter the bodies of people. Nor will the sorcerers be able to enslave and torture the souls and bodies of people who have died so that they have more power.

God will reign on earth. All people will live harmoniously with each other, respecting and loving each other. They will not make sorceries, nor will they do injustice or oppress other people. It will be paradise on earth. God will enforce this with justice, but also with punishment for those who wrong and oppress other people.

No one should think that harming the person who writes this book by God's dictation can stop God's reign on earth. He chose this person to incarnate, but his reign will continue even after that person's physical death.

God will do everything to bring paradise to earth. He will give people security, knowledge to overcome problems, and joy to enjoy this life. Hunger, misery, and oppression will end. Justice, love, and the joy of life will have taken their place.

He wants people to be right with Him so that He can give them His blessing. God gives his blessing to righteous people. When a person is not righteous with God, he cannot be righteous with anyone. He wants all people to be righteous with him so they can have his blessing.

He wants us to have love. Love is a necessary ingredient of paradise. Without love, paradise does not exist. He wants to give a gift to people; he wishes to give them his love. A person has God's love if he has a love for his fellow man, if he has a love for God, if he has a love for his mate, and if he has a love for animals. If a man has all these things, then he has the love of God.

He wants people to love truly, not falsely. To truly love means to have faith, patience, and forgiveness. When a person has all these, he truly loves.

Wants all people to have food, water, and shelter. A state should first provide these basic goods to all its citizens and then, depending on the work and abilities of each person, have more goods.

These three basic goods are given to people by God, and he wants all people to have a house for them and their family to live in and enough food and water.

He does not want people to be forced to work like slaves; he wants work to be a source of joy for people. A source of joy because he offers to his fellow man, a source of joy because he offers to society.

There is no work that does not contribute to society as a whole, and there is no work that cannot be a source of joy for the one who does it. As long as it is not done under oppression. When work is forced on a man, he rebels and does not want to work. Every man must love his work.

Every human being has the need to work, to create, and to contribute to society; it is not necessary to impose it on him. Through our work and contribution to society, we can feel fulfillment, satisfaction, and joy.

There are no jobs that contribute to society and others that do not; all jobs contribute to society, and all are necessary.

If people stop doing injustices and oppressing other people, then God will stop making floods, earthquakes, tornadoes, and droughts. All the plains will become fertile, and there will be enough food and water for all. The various epidemics will stop, and so will the diseases. People will live to a ripe old age without suffering from diseases.

Many times, the various diseases are from Satan. Almost all mental illnesses are caused by Satan. Satan, as soon as he gets an opportunity, does harm to people's souls and bodies. That is why it is important for children to be baptized as soon as possible after birth to have protection from Satan.

Once a child is baptized, Satan cannot put a demon in his body, at least not until he is eighteen years old. After that age, it is up to him or her whether Satan will be able to put a demon into his body.

A child who is not baptized as soon as he is born risks a demon, i.e., a sorcerer who has died, entering the child's body and living with him until he drives him to madness or death.

Satan wants to do harm to the souls and bodies of people because that is how he gains more power. He feeds on injustice, hatred, greed, and his need to dominate everyone and everything.

Satan does not love justice. He has no respect for people; he intends to dominate them and do whatever he wants to them. God will fight Satan by any means necessary. He will not let him dominate the earth, nor will He let him harm the souls and bodies of men.

God wants to defeat Satan, and so does the church. God needs the help of the church to defeat Satan, as well as the help of people all over the world.

Protection from demons

Any man who has a demon in his body, if he says Our Father in a normal voice fourteen times for six consecutive Fridays, then the demon will leave him.

People who do not have a demon but want protection against demons can also say this prayer. When we say this prayer, we should stand with the icon of St. Joseph and Christ facing us.

If a child has not been baptized immediately after birth. And the parents are concerned that the child may have a demon (parents should only be concerned if the child's behavior is very strange). In that case, both parents can say Our Father together fourteen times for six consecutive Fridays, in the same way that God describes above. When the demon is gone from the child's body, the child's behavior will change for the better.

Parents should not be afraid; they should treat their children with love, and under no circumstances should they beat them. If a child has a serious problem, parents should consult their doctor or a specialist and, at the same time, say this prayer. If the child's difficulty is because of a demon, by saying this prayer for six consecutive Fridays, the demon will leave the child, and his behavior will improve.

It is good that the child is in the same house when the parents say this prayer. If this is not possible, the parents can hold a photo of the child in their hands. If the child has one parent, another person who loves the child can replace the missing parent. If a child is an orphan, two people who care for and love the child can say the same prayer.

Two great inventions

God will give two big inventions to men. The first invention will be an apparatus that will provide free electricity for all the needs of the home. This invention works with the force of gravity and does not cost a lot of money to build. Its dimensions are about 1×1 meter. God will make this invention soon.

This invention, if built in larger dimensions, can provide even more power to meet the electricity needs of a neighborhood or a city. If made in smaller dimensions, it can be fitted inside a car and provide enough energy for its movement. This device would provide free electricity day and night.

No human could ever have built this device. Its dimensions are the same as those of the universe. The universe is made in the same dimensions to defeat the force of gravity. This device is a miniature of the universe.

The second invention that he wants to give people is a shell with which they will be able to fly and go from one place to another by the force of magnetic attraction. Without the use of any kind of fuel. This invention is the well-known flying saucers, or UFOs, that we have all heard of or seen in photographs.

God has already helped the people on the two other planets that exist in the universe to have this invention, and now He intends to give it to people on earth.

This construction is not difficult to build and does not require a lot of money, but it has to be built by special scientists to get it right. This invention can become a reality for the earth within a few years.

God wants to write the laws that will apply to this invention so that people will know what they will have to do if they want to use it in the future.

For this shell to be able to fly, it will have to have God's blessing. He will only bless the devices that belong to people who do not oppress, wrong, or make sorceries on other people.

This structure will not be able to collide with another structure or object that is in the air or on the ground. People who use this structure will not need any technical knowledge to be able to fly in that way.

All they will have to do is sit in it, mentally pray to God for a few seconds, and humbly and respectfully ask Him to take them to where they want to go.

Each structure will belong to one person, who would not be able to lend it, and he could not use it to transport people who do not belong to his family. Anyone who lends this device to another person will have God's punishment, and this device will not work for the person who borrowed it. If anyone tries to steal or borrow this device secretly, he or she will have God's punishment, and this device will not work.

If a person uses this device and suddenly, one day, it doesn't start to take him where he wants to go, that will mean that he has committed a serious sin. And he needs to repent, confess it to a priest, and, of course, not repeat the sin he committed in order for God to allow him to fly in that way again. This device will not be able to be used by people under the age of fifteen except with their parents.

This invention cannot be used for anything other than to travel with safety in the air. Anyone who tries to use this invention to harm, oppress, or control other people will have God's punishment, and it will stop working for that person. This invention should never be used for military purposes.

God will give people all the knowledge of what exists on other planets and universes. He will also give them the possibility to visit them in the future if they'd like with this invention. This ability to visit other planets and universes with this construction will only be given to humans when paradise has come to earth, which means that people will have gained justice, love, and balance.

God has given us a planet that can offer us everything. The earth can become our paradise without wars, injustices, or oppression. People should not worry that the population of the earth will increase too much or that there will not be enough food for everyone. If people stop making sorceries, oppressing, and wronging other people, then God will give enough food and water to all people.

It is God's job to regulate how many people will be born on earth, not the various governments. Governments should be elected by the people and should serve them, not oppress them, wrong them, or try to control their personal lives. God wants all people to be free to do whatever they want, as long as they do not limit the freedom of other people.

If a government does not respect its citizens, He will not help that government and all those responsible. A government's responsibility is huge to the people who elected it and to God, who sees and knows everything.

God has made man. He knows every little detail about the human body. He knows where all diseases come from and will share that knowledge in another book.

Since the beginning of the creation of the world, God has incarnated Himself in various healers to help people directly as well. Always by natural means. Thus, God has gained vast experience and knowledge of how various diseases can be cured naturally. And also from which major organ of the body each disease originates.

The three laws of God that, if we apply, the earth can be saved

Justice, love, and balance are the three laws of God. These laws apply to each person individually, apply to different groups, and apply to all the countries of the world. The same laws also apply to the entire universe.

Justice is the first and most important law of God. God loves this law, and on this law, the other two laws are based. If we do not have justice, we cannot have love or balance in our lives.

God's justice is not to do to other people what we would not want other people to do to us. And our punishment if we do something bad to someone will be proportional to the wrong we have done.

Love, God's second-most important law, should be our guide in every work we have to do. *Love is to behave towards other people as we would like other people to behave towards us.* Hate is from Satan. God can be angry, but he does not hate people, even the most evil, even Satan, so he is ready to forgive people who sincerely repent. When we have love, God helps us; otherwise, he cannot help us.

Balance is the third most important law of God. The entire universe relies on balance. Every task we have to do must be done with balance. *We have balance only if we apply the first two laws. If we do not apply both of the first two laws, then we cannot have balance.*

Balance is God's. He has made the entire universe with balance. The planets and the entire universe obey God's laws. God wants the people on earth to gain balance too; then paradise will have come to earth.

God wants children to be happy

God says that children have the right to be happy. For a child to be happy, he must feel loved by his parents and teachers. He must feel safe, he must feel unique, and he must feel that he is not being oppressed.

When all these things are present, a child can feel happy. Children have come into the world to be happy and to have the opportunity to live a new life; we should not oppress them, as is the case in some countries, and require them to work more hours than the adults.

While we have established the eight-hour workday for the adults, there is nothing similar for the children. As a result, if we add the hours they work at school and the hours they work at home, there are more hours that a child has to work than an adult.

The total hours a child should work should not exceed a total of seven hours per day. This working time is reasonable for a child up to the age of fifteen. After this age, children may work a little longer. Moreover, adults work five days a week and have their weekends free, while for children, we require them to study on weekends as well, giving them work to do at home.

Children should have leisure time to play games that allow them to move. A child who does not have enough leisure time to play games that involve movement together with other children is more likely to get sick with diabetes, obesity, or depression.

Furthermore, when we burden children with many hours of work at school and at home, it causes them stress, which takes a toll on their mental and physical health. There are countries that do not force children to work many hours, and that is a good thing. God wants all countries to gradually take steps in this direction.

Breastfeeding is a gift from God, and all children should breastfeed up to the age of six months. After this age, breastfeeding should stop because it benefits neither the child nor the mother.

Parents should not force children to eat; if a child does not have an appetite to eat, then it has some problem with its health.

Homosexuality, according to God, is not a sin. It is because of a hormonal imbalance. People who have this issue should not provoke others with their behavior, but other people also should not treat them as if they have done something wrong.

God cannot bless a marriage between two people of the same sex, but He does not consider it a sin if two people of the same sex live together in the same house. When paradise comes to earth, this issue will also gradually disappear.

The birth of children should take place naturally and without medication. Nature, i.e., God, has foreseen that everything should happen naturally and without the intervention of doctors. Only in cases of serious complications during birth should the doctor intervene.

God will not help doctors who administer drugs for no good reason or perform cesarean sections for their convenience or profit. The position of the woman giving birth should not prevent natural childbirth. The woman's posture should be standing or sitting in a chair, as it is most comfortable for her, and her feet should touch the floor. If a mother is lying down, this prevents her from having a natural birth.

In finishing this second book, God wants to write something about the person who is writing this book and also about his teacher, St. Joseph Buck Phong. His Second Coming could not have come, nor could paradise on earth have become a reality, if it were not for these two people. That is why God loves them and will protect them by any means.

GOD LOVES AND GETS ANGRY

God loves people because He has made them in His image and likeness. He wants them to be happy. He also loves the animals and plants.

God has feelings, like people do. He can feel anger, love, sadness, joy, and all the other emotions that humans can feel. God's heart is like a little child's heart.

God gets angry when he sees people sneakily doing sorceries on other people. He gets angry when he sees people abusing their position to oppress or wrong other people.

He gets angry when he sees leaders oppressing their people. Furthermore, he gets angry when he sees young children forced to work like slaves in school and at home. It gets angry when it sees women being given drugs for no reason to give birth or made to undergo cesarean sections for the convenience of doctors or for profit.

He gets angry when he sees people being tortured, wronged, and disrespected of their divine nature. He gets angry when he sees large rainforests being destroyed by people for profit or supposedly for the livelihood of the people living in the area. Furthermore, he gets angry when he sees animals being tortured for fun or for easy profit.

He gets angry when he sees people torturing other people; he gets angry when he sees young children, men, or women being raped. He gets angry when he sees people being treated like slaves. He gets angry when he sees women or young children being sexually exploited; he gets angry when he sees the genitals of young girls being mutilated.

God gets angry when it sees people, out of greed, oppressing and wronging other people; it gets angry when it sees an army invading another country; it gets angry when it sees a nation suffering from the invasion and occupation of another country.

God, through this book, decided to make his incarnation to Petros known, as he had made his incarnation to Christ known. For this reason, God protects Petros very well because He does not want anyone to blame him for what God dictates to him.

Satan and organized crime will not prevail on earth, nor will injustice or lies. God decided to incarnate Himself in Petros and dictate this book to him because he wants to bring paradise to earth.

When paradise comes to the earth, God will be happy because all people throughout the earth will be happy. God wants people to believe this book because then God will know that Satan will never enslave the earth.

If Satan were to enslave the earth, then God would destroy it. The destruction of the earth may come if people do not believe this book. God wants paradise to come to earth so that people can enjoy life, love, and freedom. When people rejoice, God also rejoices.

If that were possible, he would rather not punish anyone, in this life or the other, but occasionally, he can't avoid that. Punishing some people can help them change their behavior and avoid the most severe punishment, which is hell.

He wants to help people be saved from hell. He wishes to help them experience paradise on earth; that's why he decided to make his Second Coming. God loves the earth and the people. That is why he will never let Satan enslave the souls and immaterial bodies of men.

No father would ever leave his child enslaved, nor would he let him suffer from sorceries. No father would let his children suffer under dictatorships, and no father would make promises he could not keep. God is the father of all men. He would not make all the promises that he makes in this book if he could not keep them.

God does not want to let Satan make life on earth a hell. He will not let Satan dominate people and do whatever he wants to them. Nor does he want to let Satan literally enslave the souls and bodies of people who die so that he can have more power. Satan can accomplish this by doing sorceries on people while they are alive and immediately after their death.

Sorceries are the worst form of injustice and oppression. Sorceries are a way of inflicting injustice and oppression on people without the people themselves knowing that they are being wronged and oppressed. This is why God gets angry when He sees other people being wronged and oppressed with sorceries. God does not want people to make sorceries because it is like making sorceries on God himself.

He wants all people to live harmoniously with each other without killing, raping, doing wrong, oppressing, or doing sorceries. He wants all people to feel like brothers and sisters with each other because that's the way it is. God cannot tolerate the earth becoming a prison, nor can he tolerate the earth becoming the kingdom of organized crime.

He wants balance. He cannot accept hatred, falsehood, and imbalance. Furthermore, he wants justice; he cannot accept injustice and oppression. God wants happiness. If a person is oppressed and wronged, neither can God have happiness.

God wants all people all over the earth to believe in this book and love it, so he is careful about every sentence he writes. Petros could not have written this book by himself because it contains the wisdom and knowledge of God.

God tested Petros before he decided to dictate this book to him. Petros went through many trials before God decided to trust him. Not even one word in this book is from Petros.

If Petros wrote even one word without God's dictation, He would immediately stop dictating to him and punish him. Petros has promised God to write what He dictates to him. God, and only God, decides what he will write in this book.

All men have the same father, namely, God. God has his children, whom he loves all the same. If the father is angry with one of his children, it does not mean that he does not love them. He wants to help his child get back on the right path; that is why he punishes him.

God's punishment differs from man's punishment because it is done with justice, love, and balance. Justice exists because God's punishment is proportional to the evil we have done. Love exists because God is ready to forgive a person who sincerely repents. Repenting sincerely means I realize the wrong I have done, feel guilty about it, confess it to a priest, and, of course, do not repeat the same sin. The balance exists because there is justice and love.

God does not want people to have the idea that if they do something bad, He will punish them. He wants them to have the idea that if they do something bad, they will self-punish themselves. God doesn't want people to waste their energy lying, hurting, or oppressing other people.

When a person dies, both his soul and his body leave the physical body of the person who has died. The body that leaves with the soul cannot be seen because it is immaterial, but it is the normal body of the person with all the senses and emotions.

After God's judgment, the person who has died goes to paradise, purgatory, or hell. Purgatory is the opportunity God gives us to realize and repent of our sins. In purgatory, we stay five to ten years, and then we go to paradise, i.e., return to earth. When we return to earth, we stay close to God for ten to fifteen years before we are born again.

When a child is born on earth, his parents, teachers, and other people should not treat him as a person who knows nothing. Children know and understand more than we think. Every child has lived many lives and has accumulated many experiences that help him know and understand. Teachers should not treat children as if they know nothing; they should help them develop their creativity, confidence, and need to know.

Every child's need to know comes from his nature, i.e., from God. If we exploit this need of children and require them to spend excessive hours reading at school and at home, then their natural need to learn becomes a compulsion. Their drive to create and their self-confidence are diminished to a minimum.

Parents and teachers, by their example, must teach children to respect each other. Every child should feel loved by their parents and teachers without having to work endless hours every day to earn their love.

Parents should not have excessive demands from their children regarding the profession they will follow when they grow up. They should let the children choose the profession they would like to pursue. All professions are useful to society, and all professions contribute to society, as long as they are done with love by the person doing it.

God has written that the earth is in danger from Satan and organized crime, and he wants to explain this. In one country, organized crime has managed, with the assistance of Satan, i.e., sorcerers, to control almost everything. And this same organization is threatening to do the same in all the countries of the world by working with all the sorcerers and all the witches in every country. God will punish not only the people who belong to this organization but also all those who cooperate with this organization.

This organization is the most dangerous that has ever existed on earth because it does not kill with guns or bombs but with sorceries. That doesn't mean they don't have guns or that they never kill with guns, but their main weapon is sorceries. In every country, there is a group of these people. And by paying the various sorcerers in each country, they use sorceries to blackmail, murder, or exploit any person they want.

If God had not decided to make His Second Coming, they would have dominated the whole earth in a few years. Sorcerers and witches love them because they give them money to do sorceries. So do other people who are not sorcerers; they love and support them because they get money from them for various services and favors.

No man and no government can stop them because they don't seem to be doing anything wrong. The only one who can stop them is God, and He has decided to do that even if they succeed in harming the physical body of this man who is writing this book.

Planet Earth has never faced a greater threat and never will. That is why God has decided to make his Second Coming now and make his incarnation known to the person writing this book by his dictation.

If these two individuals—the teacher of the person writing this book and his disciple—had not existed, God would not have been able to incarnate. Then, in order for Satan not to prevail on earth, he would have had to cause such great natural disasters that all people on earth would have died. Except for a small group of people who would have been God's chosen ones to begin a new cycle of life on earth.

God wants to write in this book what would happen if He decided to destroy the whole earth. When He decides to destroy the entire earth, He does not just make a great flood; He makes such great natural disasters that all the infrastructure and civilization that people have built go into the bowels of the earth. The small group of people who survive will have to start building everything from scratch again.

Only a small piece of land that God has decided in advance will not go into the bowels of the earth. On this tiny piece of land live the people selected by God to survive the new cycle of life on earth. These people are no more than a few dozen, and they must certainly be good and righteous and not do witchcraft. For God to get to the point of deciding to bring paradise to earth again, thousands of years must have passed.

If God is forced to destroy the entire world, people will have to wait thousands of years before He decides again to bring paradise to earth. Because it wants people to have built the necessary infrastructure and civilization and also to get to know the difference between good and evil.

That is why God is trying so hard to bring paradise to earth now so that He does not have to destroy it. God is asking for people's help. People can help God by believing in this book. People have a unique opportunity now, within a few years, to have the paradise that God promised them long ago. The paradise that God has promised will be here on earth.

If people ignore this book and Satan prevails on earth, then God will have no choice but to destroy the whole earth.

He loves people. He will never leave them at the hands of Satan.

If God succeeds in bringing paradise to the earth now, then He will never destroy it. There will be paradise forever. God does not ask much from people to be able to bring paradise to earth. All he asks is that we be good and just with other people and with God.

God made man in his image and likeness and gave him the ability to create, i.e., to be able to make matter out of nothing. Sorcerers and witches take advantage of this ability that God has given humans to make sorceries to harm other people. God will send all sorcerers and witches to hell for abusing this ability that He has given people.

God has given this ability to people to co-create with him and not to do witchcraft. People can co-create with Him when they pray to God and ask for his help.

People will be able to co-create with Him when they pray to God to fill the three containers of basic food items. They will be able to co-create with Him when they pray to Him to give them a house made only of natural materials. They will be able to co-create with Him when they pray to Him to give them water from the sun. People will be able to co-create with God as long as they have justice, love, and balance.

The peace of God

God wants peace. Peace is God's. He loves people who want peace. He wants to give his peace to the entire world. People have lived so many years within war that they have forgotten what peace is.

Peace is living without having to work like a slave. Peace is not to want to oppress other people or do injustice to them; peace is not to want to hurt anyone; peace is not to care what your neighbor has.

Furthermore, peace is not wanting glory; peace is not wanting more and more; and peace is not worrying about what comes tomorrow. Peace is having security; peace is having enough food and water and a house to live in even if you are not working. He will give all these things to people so they should not have anxiety and insecurity. They should have peace.

God wants to give people glory. God's glory is justice, love, and balance. When a person has these, then he has glory. Glory is measured by how good a person is.

He would like to give people respect. When people respect their fellow man, then they will have respect.

He wants to give love to people. When people have a love for their fellow man, then they will have love. God wants all people to have money, glory, respect, and love. He wants all people to have these things so that God can have them, too.

God does not want glory to be glorified but to help people; he does not want respect to be respected but so that he can respect people. He does not want love so that he can be loved, but he wants love so that he can love people. He wants all people to love him so that he can love them too. Furthermore, he wants all people to pray to God so that he can help them.

The paradise on earth

When paradise comes, the earth will have two suns so that there will be sunshine everywhere. All the ice will melt without causing the slightest disappearance of land. He will keep the temperature konstant at 25 degrees Celsius throughout the earth. People will have enough food and water because God will make the whole earth fertile.

He will make people his co-creators. People will be able to pray to Him, and He will give them food. Each person will be able to have three metal containers in his house, and God will fill those three containers with food as soon as they are empty.

Each person will be able to fill the first two containers with legumes of his choice and put meat or fish in the third. The container with meat or fish, after filling it, will then have to be emptied, and the contents stored in the refrigerator.

Once these containers are almost empty, people will be able to pray to God, and God will fill them according to the contents of each container.

The contents of the third container, which will be meat or fish, and we will have kept it in the refrigerator when it is about to run out. We should put some of it in the empty container and pray so that God will fill it as He did with the other two containers.

God had done this miracle together with Christ two thousand years ago, when Christ had fed a great many people with the little food He had.

He will make this miracle for every person who will pray to him and ask him for it, as long as they have justice, love, and balance. He must also be baptized as a Christian and be good and just with all people.

Furthermore, he will also give a home to every man who needs one for himself and his family. He will also give safety to people and knowledge to enjoy life. He wants people to experience paradise on earth in this life cycle and not in the next.

God wants people to believe in this book so that he can bring paradise to earth within a few years. And not wait thousands of years for the earth to be ready again to have paradise on earth. He does not ask much of people. The most basic thing is to be kind and just to their fellow man and not do sorceries.

The destruction of the earth

God has been forced twice before in the past to destroy the whole earth. The first time a king with the power of arms had enslaved the entire earth. And the second time, another country, Atlantis, again with the power of arms, conquered the entire earth.

This time, the earth is not threatened by the power of arms but by organized crime, which, together with Satan, i.e., the sorcerers and witches, threatens to take over the entire earth. God does not want to scare people. He wants to tell them the truth.

It would be much worse for people if Satan enslaved their souls and bodies than for them to die and go to paradise, i.e., to return to earth and live a new life. He will never let Satan dominate the earth. The earth is his creation, and so is man, and he loves them.

The interpretation of Our Father

Another subject God wants to write about is Our Father. Our Father is the prayer that God dictated to Christ, and now He wants to explain that prayer.

Our Father is literally a prayer that speaks of God's reign on earth, and when He reigns on earth, His will shall be done. His will is to bring paradise to earth so that all people can be happy and joyful.

Our Father is the phrase with which God begins this prayer. He is actually the father of all people because He has created them. He wants people to call him their father and to feel him like their father because that is the truth.

God will give us the daily bread. The daily bread is the wisdom and truth God gives through this book.

His forgiveness is given to us if we sincerely repent. Our forgiveness to other people is given if we do not seek to repay the evil but pray to God and ask for his help.

Temptation is nothing more than not following the Ten Commandments.

The evil one that we ask God to save us from is Satan. God wants to help people be saved from Satan.

That is what God is also doing through this book. God dictated this prayer to Christ so that people would know the truth about Him. Our Father is the most powerful prayer because it is from God.

God gets angry when he sees Satan making movies, ostensibly to entertain children. And in reality, what he is really doing is making witchcraft, scaring them, and telling them how good sorcerers and witches are, i.e., Satan. Children's movies sometimes contain sorceries. Parents should not allow their children to watch movies that scare them because Satan can then more easily harm them. He will not allow Satan to continue to do this. He will punish anyone who makes movies that contain sorceries for children or adults.

God gets angry when He sees people making horror or extreme violence movies for either young children or adults. Violence scares people, makes them more aggressive towards other people, and takes away their power. These feelings are more intense in children. People should avoid watching such films.

He also gets angry when he sees films made that contain sexual violence against children or women. Sexual violence is one of the worst forms of violence because it involves a very sensitive area of human life. A person who watches a film of child pornography or sexual violence against children or adults tends to want to do the same in his or her own personal life. That is why he will punish those who make such films. The same applies to those who distribute child pornography material or sexually exploit children.

Another issue that God wants to speak about is the destruction of the Amazon forest. That is where all the gold of the earth is found—the most precious trees that give life to the entire world. The Amazon forest must remain as it is because it is important to the earth's ecosystem.

Another issue that angers Him is when people who are with Satan, i.e., they are sorcerers, ask Him for help with health problems they may have. God cannot help a person who is doing sorceries; he must first repent, stop doing sorceries and confess so that He can help him.

God has decided to do many miracles, but He will never do a miracle for someone who is a sorcerer. Nor will he make a miracle for an evil man. God will only do these miracles in the church and never outside it. Any person who wants a miracle from Him should come to the church.

The church is God's. He loves her and wants to help her become stronger. He wants all people all over the earth to believe in the church and in God's power and love for people. If it were not for the church, He would not have a place for people to worship Him, ask for His help, and for Him to give it to them with joy.

Another thing that He does not like is when people ask for help, and when He helps them, people forget to thank Him. And do not even acknowledge that the help they asked for was given to them by God. God doesn't ask for vows or to burn big candles for him. But he wants to hear a thank-you in our prayer and the realization that the help we received was not accidental but from God.

This way, God sees that we have acknowledged the help he has given us, and the next time we ask for his help, he will run to help us. If we forget to say even a thank you, then he will not help us the next time we ask for his help.

Another thing he doesn't like is when people can't tell Satan from God. Satan wants to harm people's souls and bodies, wants to dominate them with his sorceries, wants to take their souls and bodies when they die, and his goal is to govern the whole earth. Satan's characteristics are hatred, injustice, greed, and his need to control everyone and everything. God is love, justice, and forgiveness.

God loves people; he has made them in his image and likeness and wants them to have freedom. But on the other hand, he cannot let Satan wrong, oppress, or do whatever he wants to people with sorceries. He will punish Satan; he will not let him prevail on earth.

People will be able to enjoy life. Sorceries, injustice, and oppression will stop; wars will stop. He will give enough food and water to all. Life on earth will become their paradise. Every person reading this book should be able to distinguish whether it is from God or from Satan. The same is true of the miracles that He will do. Satan can do sorceries, but he can never do miracles.

Another issue that he does not like is when representatives of the church do not believe in God's Second Coming on earth. That is, they do not believe in His love for people and His power. The church believes that God's Second Coming will be for God to destroy the earth and that paradise will be somewhere else, but not on earth. God has never said that He will destroy the earth and that paradise will be somewhere else. The only thing he has said is that "good people will go to paradise".

God loves the Catholic and Orthodox churches because they both have the sacrament of Holy Communion. Both churches are equal, and God wants one church to not blame the other. He wants the two churches to cooperate and not compete. He also wants, if possible, these two churches to unite in the future.

One church should not be considered superior to the other because God loves both of these churches equally. He wants all churches to have the sacrament of Holy Communion so that he can help them. The priests should respect the people, and the people should respect the priests. God is just, and He wants the church to be just to the people and also to the priests.

He also wants the church to have money so that it can help people in need. God does not want the church to be poor and without power. He wants the church to have power. The church must not squander this power, nor must it abuse it. Wants justice, love, and balance. The same is true for the church.

Priests must be fair to all people, but especially to the most vulnerable and children. He wants children to have understanding and love from the church and give them time to mature.

The Second Coming of God

God decided to make his incarnation in Christ known to teach people how to treat their fellow human beings, and now he is making his incarnation in the person writing this book also known to bring paradise to earth. If people want proof of this from God, they can ask for whatever proof they want, and He will give it to them.

A great proof would be to ask God to make it rain in Greece for a certain period of time. Another great proof would be to ask Him to find children or adults who are missing or abducted in any area of the earth. God will do many miracles for people to believe in this book. He wants us to be fair to other people, but also fair to him.

The laws of God

God wants the laws He writes in this book to have power, and that's why He puts everything He writes into the basic laws, which are justice, love, and balance.

He wants justice because, without justice, there is no love or balance. Wants love because without love, there is no justice or balance. He wants balance because, without balance, there is no justice or love. He wants justice because he is just. He wants love because he is love. He wants balance because he is balance.

He wants all or nothing. He wants paradise on earth or the destruction of the earth; he wants justice or the destruction of the earth; he wants love or the destruction of the earth. Furthermore, he wants balance or the destruction of the earth. God wants all or nothing, so he is not afraid of organized crime. If organized crime prevails on earth, He will destroy the earth so that a new cycle of life on earth can begin.

Sorcerers and witches will go to hell, and so will the members of the mafia. God wants to bring paradise to earth. He cannot let the members of a criminal organization dominate the earth. The members of this criminal organization, with Satan's help, want to enslave the earth. They have already succeeded in one country, and now they intend to do the same to the entire earth.

He wants freedom. He cannot tolerate the earth becoming a prison, nor can he tolerate the earth becoming a kingdom of mobsters and sorcerers. Wants balance. He cannot accept hatred, falsehood, and imbalance. He wants justice; he cannot accept injustice and oppression.

The ways God helps people

Another thing he does not like is when people want him to help them without doing anything themselves. He can help a person who is trying to do something, but if a person is not trying at all, God cannot help him.

There are many ways that he can help someone. One way that God helps people is by giving them both mental and physical strength to cope with a task or problem. Another way is by helping them think of a solution to an issue they are having to deal with. Yet another way he helps people is by punishing people who have wronged them.

Sending someone who can help them is another way to do that. Another way is when He helps them through a dream; yet another way is when He helps them with a health issue; yet another way is when God decides to tell the truth to a person through a written message, which He will send to that person through another person who communicates with God.

This last way is the way He has chosen to help people throughout the world. This book is the message he wants to send to all people on earth.

God would not have decided to make His Second Coming if there was no real threat from Satan. Within a few years, Satan would have dominated the entire earth with the assistance of organized crime. The only solution for God would be to destroy the entire world and begin a new cycle of life. People must decide what they want: God to prevail on earth or Satan to prevail.

GOD AND MONEY

God wants all people to know the truth about money. Money is an invention of man. Money goes to the people who love it. When a person earns money honestly, that is not bad, but when he earns money by oppressing or wronging other people, he is serving Satan.

Satan wants people to earn money by doing injustices or oppressing other people because then he knows those people are on his side. Satan is nothing more than the sorcerers and witches all over the world, as God has already mentioned. He will punish people who make money by wronging or oppressing other people in a systematic and repeated manner.

God's punishment for these people will be harsh. These people will not be able to enjoy their money. He will take all the joy of life away from these people. They will not be able to enjoy sex, food, or the material possessions that they have.

He will do this so that these people will realize that what they are doing is not right and repent. He will forgive these people if they repent and stop doing these bad things. God wants to bring paradise on earth; He cannot let people oppress, wrong, or make sorceries against other people.

God will punish those who practice sorceries to make money. The punishment that He will do to these people if they do not repent will be death and hell.

God wants all people to be able to enjoy money and not to be a source of stress for people. People can achieve this through righteousness, love, and balance.

Justice is essential in every transaction we have with the other people. Justice, the first and most important law of God, must be applied in every transaction with another person. He will punish the people who do not apply this first law, and his punishment will be proportional to the harm they have caused the other person.

Love, the second most significant law of God, must be present in every transaction with other people. Love exists when we respect other people, respect their work, or respect the product they have given us. The same is true of the one who does some work or gives a product to another person.

Balance, the third most essential law of God, exists only if the first two laws are present. Without justice, we cannot have balance. The same is true if we do not have love.

God says that people should never give money to Satan. When we give money to Satan to do sorceries, we give him our soul. The same is true if we give in to Satan's blackmail, and to stop him from casting spells on us, we give him money.

If a person is blackmailed by Satan in this way and prays to God, then God will help that person by giving him strength but also punish Satan very harshly. He says that we should have our money where our soul is. Our souls should never be with Satan.

The money that every man has should not be wasted. If a person wastes his money, he is actually wasting his life. With money, we can get what we need and want, but we should never waste it. Wasting is from Satan. Satan wants people to waste their money, that is, to waste their power. When a man wastes his money, i.e., his power, Satan can more easily harm him.

The same applies to food. We must not waste it. God says that the food we eat is from God, and we should love it and not waste it. He does not want us to waste food, nor does God want us to waste our lives. He wants all people to love their lives but also the lives of other people.

Inside our house, it is not good to have marble because Satan can do easier sorceries on us. Furthermore, for the same reason, it is not good to have a fig tree planted in our garden or on our sidewalk. Another thing we should not have inside our house are plants that smell strongly, such as gardenias and magnolias. Another thing we should not put in our house is the color yellow. The color yellow is the color of death, and Satan takes advantage of this to make us sorceries.

Sorceries are the most dangerous way of blackmailing and murdering people because they are done without anyone realizing it. We should never complain to a person who, we think, has done us harm. First, we are uncertain if it is that person, and second, if we complain, we give that person more power to hurt us.

God knows which person tried to hurt us and will punish them if we pray to him. The punishment God will give to the person who tried to hurt us will be proportional to the harm they tried to do to us.

Another issue he wants to talk about is illegal immigration. Immigrants who come to a country must respect the laws, the way of life, and the people of that country. People who come to a country illegally should not think that they are coming to that country as conquerors but as people who are asking the country they have entered illegally to help them have a better life.

Each country can accept a certain number of immigrants. If the number of immigrants that a country accepts is too high, then the standard of living of the people living in that country is degraded.

If a country neighboring Greece does nothing but rather facilitates migrants crossing its territory and entering Greece illegally, then God will punish that country. If the same country violates Greece's airspace daily, then God will punish it.

If the same country has enslaved another island country for decades, then God will punish that country. If the same country tries to make war on Greece, then God will punish that country very severely.

He does not want any country to invade another country, nor does he want a country to threaten another country with war. If that same country had enslaved Greece for four hundred years and, with God's help, was freed, then He would not let Greece be enslaved by that same country again.

God would not have been able to help the Greeks be liberated from the Turks if they had not believed in God. The same is true for the Israelites; he could not have helped them be delivered from the ancient Egyptians if they did not believe in God. God will do the same for all the countries in the world. He will not leave any country to be enslaved by another country.

Greece is a country that respects its neighbors, and its neighbors must do the same towards Greece. If there weren't the people of Greece to welcome my teacher, Joseph Buck Phong. Neither I would have had the chance to meet a teacher who would have given me all the means and helped me in order for God to incarnate in me.

My teacher, with God's help, had healed prime ministers, the president of the republic, and hundreds of thousands of people with acupuncture and natural food supplements. He had never advertised, but people were going to him because they loved him and were happy with the healing he did for them.

He never deceived anyone, he always respected all people, and he never wanted to give even one more treatment to a person than he really needed to get more money. If he was not truly righteous, God would not have helped him do the healings he did, nor would he have made him a saint right after his death.

Satan, with the assistance of organized crime, as has been mentioned, has managed to control a significant number of people in one country. He knows how to do it, and now he is trying to do the same all over the earth. If it were not for God, he would have prevailed over all the earth.

God will stop Satan and save the earth. If he had not been able to incarnate, he would not have been able to save the earth. This person's teacher was giving lessons to his students with God's help. He did not stop giving lessons even when he was seriously ill, hoping that one of his students would be able to continue his work.

When he saw that his disciple was ready and that God would be able to incarnate in him, he prayed to God to continue the work of teaching to his disciple. He himself, because of his health problem, would have to leave this life. Satan continued to slander him even after his death.

The unfair trade competition

Another subject God wants to talk about is competition between businesses. The competitiveness of businesses should not come at the expense of workers' wages or working conditions.

Competitiveness among businesses in all countries of the world must be about the quality of their products, the services they give after the sale of their products, and the design or ease of use of the product.

The increase in productivity that has been achieved through machines. It must be something that will help people work in better working conditions and without oppression. Not, as has been the case so far, that machines leave people unemployed.

He wants all workers to work without oppression. Work to be for them a source of joy and not of stress, frustration, and misery. He will not help those companies that treat workers unfairly. Likewise, he will do the same for businesses that treat their customers unfairly.

God does not want a business to oppress, wrong, or do sorceries on its employees or customers. He wants all businesses around the world to have the same minimum wage, the same social security contributions, and the same taxation so that there is no unfair competition between businesses around the world.

If a business is trying to increase its sales in unfair ways, God will not help that business. If a country tries to use unfair practices to increase the competitiveness of its businesses, then it will not help that country.

Wants to bring paradise on earth, and paradise without improvement of working conditions cannot be possible. This improvement in working conditions must be done gradually by all countries; otherwise, it will not work in practice.

Every state, to provide some services to its citizens, must have some revenue. This revenue can be found by taxing its citizens. A government must be fair in taxing its citizens but also not waste this money.

Each country should consume the products it produces. The imports a country makes from another country should be of equal value to the exports it makes to that country. Two countries can trade different products that each country produces with each other, but those products must always be of equal value in money. God will make all the countries of the world fertile, and they will have enough food and water for all their citizens.

People shouldn't worry about climate change on the planet. Because all these are God's work, if people stop oppressing, doing injustice, and making sorceries against other people, then all these phenomena will stop.

He wants to bring paradise to earth so that there will be a perfect climate. The perfect climate gives joy to people. People don't get too cold or too hot, so they can be happier. Wants all people on earth to be happy.

Another theme God would like to talk about is currency. All the countries in the world should have the same currency. This would solve many problems in the transactions between countries and also save a lot of money. A single currency for all the countries of the world could help them have more understanding, solidarity, and justice among themselves. Each country could trade with other countries without worrying about currency exchange rates. And without having to put only its interests first.

Another thing God wants to talk about is communication between all the countries in the world. Every country should have its language, and there should be another international language in which people from all the countries of the world can communicate with each other. This international language should be easy to learn. It should also be spoken by many people on earth already. This is the English language.

If every person could communicate with all people on earth by learning only two languages, their mother language and another language, this would solve many communication problems between people. But it would also save a lot of money that could be used for other human needs.

Another issue that God wants to talk about is gambling. When a person gambles, it is like asking Satan to give him money. This is because we have not earned that money honestly, i.e., with our work. And second, if we win that money, someone else will have lost it.

Satan knows this, and he does many sorceries on people related to their money. We should never engage in gambling of any kind. Governments of all countries should not encourage these games. People should not seek profit at the expense of another person.

God can help all the countries of the world in various ways, but he wants each country not to be concerned only with its interests. One way in which He can help all the countries of the world is by not causing any natural disasters, as long as people stop making sorceries, doing injustices, and oppressing other people.

Another way God can help is to make the whole earth fertile. Another way is to give people knowledge to overcome problems. One more way is to help people live longer without health issues; another way is to give them safety. Another way is, if a country is confronted with a serious issue, to help her with that issue. Yet another way is to make the climate all over the earth ideal for people.

The Secret of creativity

God wants to give people the secret of creativity. People can co-create with him. Creation is God's. He creates every moment. He loves creation, and creation loves God. God has made creation. He knows how it works, and now he wishes to share the secret of creation with people.

Creation loves love. When we have love, we can create. Creation wants quietness, creation wants a clear mind, creation wants caresses, creation wants sex, creation wants time, creation wants company, creation wants a bed, creation wants a table, and creation wants a chair.

Creation wants these because man can create in all of them. Man can create in solitude and in good company; he can create sitting at the table or lying in bed. He can create wherever circumstances allow him, as long as he has love.

Love is an essential ingredient of creation. Without love, there can be no creation. Love is of God; creation is of God. God is creation and love.

God wants all people to create; he wants them to co-create with him. Man can co-create with God when he has love. God wants all people to co-create with Him. Man co-creates with God when he has sex, and a new life is born. He creates when he makes music, cooks, gardens, or writes. When he has problems he is trying to solve, when he has joy, when he has company, and when he is alone. A man can create as long as he has love.

God wants all people to trust him because that way he can help them more. He wants people to love him because that's how he can help them more. He wants people to be good and fair to their fellow men.

No man wants to be oppressed and wronged. We must also not want to oppress and wrong other people. He wants all people to love their fellow men. People must behave towards others as they would like the other people to behave towards them. He will punish people who behave toward other people without respect and dignity. His punishment will be commensurate with their offense.

The right to self-expression

God wants to talk about the right to self-expression. The right to self-expression is a key component of paradise. Paradise does not exist without the right to self-expression. People should be able to express themselves in any way they wish, as long as they do not limit the freedom of other people.

The ways a person can express himself are many. Each person chooses the way he likes to express himself. Some ways of self-expression are singing, listening to music, writing, painting, and walking in the countryside. Reading a book, riding a bicycle in the countryside, driving on a route we like, having a good conversation, having sex with our spouse, and most importantly, our work, as long as we are doing it with love.

The work of each person is the basic way through which he can express himself. In order for someone to express himself through his work, he must love it. In order for someone to love his work, it must not be oppressed and must be treated with respect and dignity. God wants all people to love their work. Employers should be fair to employees, and working conditions should be as good as possible for each employee.

Why we must have justice, love, and balance

God wants to give people a gift. His gift is the ability to have justice. We have justice when we don't want to lose our love. Love is from God. God gives his love to righteous individuals. God's love is the warmth we feel in our soul when we are righteous. If we are not righteous, we lose that warmth from our soul, i.e., we lose God's love.

He gives this warmth only to righteous people. When a person loses this warmth, he loses everything. God does this to make people realize that what they did was not right and to help them repent. God is not evil. He doesn't wish to punish people, but he wants to help them get back on the right path, God's path. If He was letting these people do unjust things to others, then the earth would have been hell long ago. He wishes to bring paradise to earth, not hell.

Another gift God would like to give people is love. Love is from God. It is one of the laws he has made for the entire universe. When we have love, God helps us; otherwise, he cannot help us. He can only help people if they have love. He wants us to have love, the love of God.

A person has love when they pray to God and ask for his help for the injustices they may have done to him instead of hating those people. Hate is from Satan. Satan wants people to hate him because then he knows he can do whatever he wants to them. One way Satan does his sorceries is to unjust people so they hate him, and then he finds an opportunity to hurt them more easily.

Another gift that God wants to give people is balance. We can only have balance if we have justice and love. If we don't have both, then we cannot have balance. Balance is from God. He wants all people to have balance. He gives balance to people through the laws he has made. If a person does not have justice and love, then he cannot have balance. This happens automatically, without God having to do anything about it. If a person wants to have balance, then he must have justice and love.

He would like to help people to have balance. That is why he decided to write this book. People need to study this book and not just read it. Every word in this book is carefully chosen because he wants people to get to know his wisdom and his knowledge.

Life after death

Another topic God wants to talk about is life after death. The life after death is nothing more than our return to earth to live a new life. Our life is the most important thing we have because it allows us to have experiences that will help us become one with God.

He wants all people to become one with him. When all people become one with Him, then the true paradise will prevail on earth. True paradise is something that people have not even imagined. The true paradise is the true God. He wants all people to live in the true paradise, i.e., the true God.

Through this book, God wants to describe what true paradise will be like. True paradise will be the opposite of true hell. People will be able to live in safety, justice, and love. No part of the earth will lack fertile valleys so that people and animals alike can have enough food and water.

No part of the earth will lack sunshine, and no part of the earth will lack an ideal climate. There will be no part of the earth that will not have a clean environment. No part of the earth will lack the shell with which every person will be able to fly and visit, with safety and no cost at all, any place on earth he wants.

People must be fair to all people. One reason they have to be fair is because they don't know in what position they will find themselves in their next life. A man who is wealthy in this life may be poor in the next. God often sends people who were rich into a poor family to have this experience as well. Especially if those people took advantage of their power to wrong and oppress other people. That is why people should be fair and kind to all people.

God has made rules according to which every person will be reborn on earth. If a man was rich in his previous life, he must be born poor to have this experience as well. A man who was poor in his previous life must be born rich to also have this experience. If a man has slept with many women, then he must have been born not so handsome that women will not like him so much. If a man has been rich and has wronged other people, then God will make him poor. And if a man had power and abused that power, then God would punish him by making him weak.

He wants to tell people that they can have as much wealth as they want. Wants all people to have wealth. God's wealth is not the same as people's wealth. God's wealth is not measured by money in the bank or pounds of gold; it is measured by justice, love, and balance.

People don't need many things to feel rich. People do need healthy food to feel rich; they need good sex with their spouse they have married in the church; they do need safety; they need justice; they need love and balance. Love and balance go together, and so does justice.

Another issue God wants to speak about is terrorism. He does not want any man to terrorize and blackmail other people to achieve his goals. If a person or a group of people believes they are being wronged, they can pray and ask for His help. He will help the person or group that is being wronged if he sees that they are really right. But not every person or group can, to achieve their goals, plant bombs, kill innocent people, and terrorize millions of others.

God will punish harshly not only the people who commit such an act of terrorism, but also those who are liable for this act. He will also punish harshly those who blackmail other people to extort money from them.

The Miracles of God

God wants to do many miracles for people to believe this book. If people believe in this book, he will be able to bring paradise to earth. One miracle God would like to do is locate people who have been kidnapped or are missing. God can find exactly where a person who has been abducted or is missing is located.

What God will do will be a miracle. No man in the world can locate where a person is who has been abducted or is missing, except God. God's essence is in every person, and that is why God can communicate with all people.

Another miracle God wants to do is to make it rain in an area of Greece if people ask him to. God can make rain in any area of Greece and for any amount of time that people ask him to.

Another issue he would like to talk about is the internet. The internet is an invention of people that allows them to communicate more easily with each other. God does not want a person over the internet to wrong, oppress, or do sorceries. He will punish those who wrong, oppress, or make sorceries through the internet. The internet can help people, but it should not be a dangerous place for children or adults. The punishment God will inflict on those who do these bad things over the internet will be commensurate with the evil they tried to do.

Another issue that God wants to talk about is the administration of justice. Judges have an obligation to be fair to all citizens. So do all the people involved in the administration of justice. In cases where a judge deliberately fails to be fair to all people, God will punish that judge and those who have deliberately contributed to an unjust decision.

The prevention of drugs

Another subject God wants to talk about is drug prevention. Young people must know the side effects of drugs so that they can decide with a clear mind whether to take them or not. They also must know a few of the reasons why people start taking drugs.

People think that if they take drugs, they will become sexually liberated. They will have more pleasure when they have sex; they will become stronger and smarter, and they won't be afraid at all.

In fact, what drugs actually do is precisely the opposite. People lose the ability to have pleasure when they have sex. They become weak mentally and physically; they can't concentrate on anything they do, and they become afraid of everyone and everything.

When children feel that their parents and teachers love and respect them, it is harder for them to take drugs. When a person takes drugs, Satan can more easily hurt him.

One way that Satan makes young people want to take drugs is by making sorceries and taking away from them the joy of life. People become unhappy without knowing why they're unhappy. When a child or adult is unhappy, it is easier for them to seek happiness in drugs.

The way Satan takes the joy of life away from people is by doing sorceries in the anus. The anus is a point that can give joy to the whole body and also to the soul. Sorcerers and witches know this and do many sorceries on this point to take the joy away from people.

When a person becomes unhappy, it is easy to resort to drugs, drinking, gambling, and anything else that could give him some artificial happiness.

Drugs and the other habits we have mentioned, such as gambling and drinking, may be considered sins. But in God's eyes, this behavior is not a sin by itself because the person is only hurting himself.

Drug prevention is the most important step. All children need to know the consequences of drugs, especially in their future sexual lives. If someone is already taking drugs, they should seek help from the experts. He can also pray to God and ask for his help.

God can help a person who takes drugs if they pray to Him daily. There are many ways that God can help. One way is to give him strength mentally and physically; another way is to help him remove the spells that Satan has put on him. Another way is to help him not be afraid, and another way is to help him with any health problems he may have.

God will punish the large-scale drug dealers. The punishment for these people will be proportional to the harm they do to people who take drugs.

God wants to warn the sorcerers and witches and tell them that God's punishment, if they do not repent, will be death. When sorcerers and witches destroy the lives of millions of people, the punishment they deserve is death. After their deaths, they will go straight to hell.

Cure for mental illnesses

God wants to help people who are suffering from a serious mental illness. Almost all mental illnesses come from Satan. Satan does sorceries on people to drive them to madness or death.

In the case of mental illness, Satan is cooperating with the demons. Demons are nothing more than witches or sorcerers who have died. Their immaterial bodies are tiny, but they have all the intelligence and wickedness they had while living in their physical bodies. They have no physical strength at all; all they can do is sorceries.

The demons enter people's physical bodies, specifically the spleen, and from there they use their sorceries to influence people's thoughts and emotions. They also make people see or hear things that don't exist.

Demons choose good people to lead them to madness or death. They have the help of other sorcerers who are still alive, and in this way, they work together to do evil to the people they choose.

When a person has been baptized as a Christian, he has protection from demons until the age of eighteen. Occasionally, however, Satan can put a demon in a child at a very young age before his parents have had the time to baptize him.

For this reason, it is best for children to be baptized within the first fifteen days of their birth to be sure that Satan has not had time to put a demon in the child.

The demons, to lead a person to madness or death, take a few years. The reason they do this is that it gives them more power.

God wants to give people a way to take out demons and cure mental illnesses. This is possible with the help of God.

Every person who has a demon in his body, if every Friday he says Our Father fourteen times in a normal voice (not mentally), the demon will leave from inside him. The person should be upright and have the icon of St. Joseph and Christ facing him.

Our Father is the most powerful prayer because it is given by God Himself. If a person says this prayer in this way for five or six Fridays, the demon will leave from inside him.

(The demon may leave the second or third time a person says this prayer, but it is better to say it for five or six Fridays to be certain.) If his illness was caused by a demon, then that person will be well after that.

If a person is so mentally ill that he cannot say Our Father fourteen times, then two people who love that person can say this prayer in the same way, holding in their hands a photo of the ill person.

When the demon is gone, that person will feel a little weak for a few days, but thereafter, he will be fine. If a person's life or health is in danger because of a serious mental illness, then he should visit his doctor, follow his doctor's instructions, and at the same time say Our Father fourteen times every Friday.

If a person is taking medication for a mental illness, he should not reduce or stop his medication without the consent of his doctor.

This prayer can also be said by people who do not have a demon or a mental illness but want protection from demons. If someone wants protection, they can say this prayer once a year for five or six consecutive Fridays.

People should not be afraid of demons, especially after the way God gives in this book for people to take out demons, either from themselves or from a person in their family. God will send the demons that come out of people's bodies straight to hell so they can't hurt other people.

The protection of children

God wants to tell parents they should never hit their children. Parents can get angry or yell at their children, but they should never hit them. When a parent hits his child, it is a sin according to God, and Satan can hurt that child more easily.

Children are not evil; they have come from paradise, so parents should protect and love them. If a parent is forced to punish his child, this punishment should not be strict.

Parents should see their children with understanding. They should pray to God and ask for his help with any problems they may have with them.

Parents need to know that a child needs to play games that involve movement together with other children to defuse. They must know that each child has lived many lives, which allows them to know and be aware of more things than the parents think.

They have to know that these children have been reborn on earth because, in their previous life, they were not bad people; otherwise, they would have gone to hell. Furthermore, they must know that they have a responsibility to each of their children, and they have to be good and fair to them.

Occasionally, a child can be naughty or sad because Satan is doing sorceries on them. Parents can pray to God and ask for his help if they have difficulties with their children.

Moreover, parents can say Our Father three times mentally with their child in mind or by looking at him or her if they think he or she may have some sorcery. Each time they say Our Father, they must add the word "amen" at the end three times. If parents say this prayer, God will immediately take out any sorceries their child may have.

Another way parents can protect their children is by telling them they love them. Parents should treat their children in a way that will make them feel like they are their ally. Another way is by putting an icon of the Holy Mary in their room, and also a cross.

When the children are a little older, if they like, they can have a small cross and a talisman hanging around their necks. With the image of St. Joseph on one side and the image of the Holy Mary on the other. Another way is to speak to their children kindly.

Children's dreams

Another way Satan harms children is through dreams. In some cases, the dreams that children have are from Satan. Satan sends these dreams to children or adults through sorceries. Parents need to reassure their children when they have scary dreams. God never sends scary dreams to children or adults. God may send a dream to an adult to help him, but He will never send them a dream that will scare them. The recurring dreams that children or adults may have are always from Satan.

God respects and loves every child. All the children of the world are children of God. When he sees a child suffering, he is sorry. He wants children to be happy and not suffer as if they are in hell.

Children's sports are necessary for every child, but when a child is oppressed to perform highly in sports, that is not good. Parents and teachers should not oppress children to perform well in sports. Sports should be a joy for children, not an oppression.

All the children of the world need God. He needs the children. Without them, God would not exist. In the same way, they would not exist without God. He helps children with any problem they may have and can do everything to help a child.

He would like every child to pray to God so that He can help them. When a child prays to Him, He always helps them. This is because God knows that every child is good. He wants all children to pray to God because God is their father. He wants children to be happy, not to fear their teachers or their parents, but to love them.

Likewise, he wants children's parents to be happy so that God can be happy, too. When people are happy, he is happy as well. God wants to bring paradise to earth so that all people can be happy. He wants the same for all children around the world.

God will give people everything they need to be happy. He will give them safety, knowledge, a perfect climate, food and water, health, and the knowledge to enjoy life.

On the other side, it will punish people who oppress, wrong, or cast spells on other people. God's promise that good people will go to paradise is about to be fulfilled.

Another issue God wants to talk about is people's safety. All people should feel safe wherever they are. He will punish those who try to hurt another person in any way. The punishment that He will do to these people will be proportional to the harm they tried to do. God's punishment for these individuals from now on will be done in a more immediate way.

God wants to impose justice on earth; He cannot let these individuals wrong, oppress, or do sorceries for their own personal gain. The security that He will give to all people is the first step in bringing the paradise on earth that He has promised.

Another issue God would like to talk about is the appearance of a promise of God. When God promises something, positive or negative, it is always done. God's promises take some time, so people should not lose faith when a promise of God takes some time to fulfill.

Occasionally, the bigger a truth is, the harder it is for people to believe it. God is not a liar, and neither is Petros. God does not want people to believe this book without any evidence. He wants people to ask for whatever proof they want so they can be convinced that this book is from God. He is ready to give whatever proof people ask for.

Another subject he wants to speak about is the truth. For there to be justice on earth, there must be truth. God will punish individuals who lie to hurt another person.

The punishment that God will inflict on a person who lied will be proportional to the harm they tried to do by lying. If God has decided to bring paradise on earth, He cannot let individuals lie intending to do harm to another person.

Another issue he wants to talk about is globalization. He wants each country to be unique and respected by its neighbors. One country should never invade another country. No country should have another country enslaved, and no country should threaten another country with war.

He also wants all countries to have a common currency, an international language, and cooperation between countries. This model of globalization will solve many problems and improve cooperation between countries.

He will not help those countries that only pursue their very own interests and not the interests of all the countries on earth. If a country is only interested in its interests and isn't concerned about the interests of other countries, it will not help that country or those who are responsible.

God wants to help Greece overcome the economic crisis. He would like to help Greece find the oil and gold in its subsoil. God can, if asked, point out exactly where in Greece there is oil or gold.

He would also like to help Greece with all its national issues because he believes Greece is right on all of them. God wants Greece to be one of the first countries to have paradise on earth. He wants to do all this because he loves Greece. Greece is a country that believes in God. He would like to do the same for every country that asks for his help, as long as that country is democratic and does not want to oppress or invade another country.

For a country to be considered democratic, there must be free elections, freedom of expression for its citizens, and freedom of the press.

The Incarnations of God

Since the beginning of the creation of the world, God has been incarnated in various people. Like every human being, he has a body. God's body is immaterial; we cannot see it.

Only on exceptional occasions does God show his immaterial body to people. In these exceptional cases, he shows his immaterial body to help a person in danger.

God has made man in his image and likeness. His body is the same as a man's body, only it is immaterial. The body of men is also immaterial when they leave their physical body after death.

God has incarnated many times in different people. One of these people was Petros' teacher, Joseph Buck Phong. God's incarnation on Petros' teacher was a secret incarnation. No one, including Petros, knew about it until after the death of his teacher.

God could never incarnate in an infant, first because the infant cannot give him permission to incarnate in it and, second, because God's energy is so great that an infant could not bear it.

God can never incarnate in a person without his permission, nor can he incarnate in someone he does not consider worthy to be incarnated.

To be worthy for God to be incarnate in him, a person must not only be good and righteous and not do sorceries but must also have been well-trained by another teacher in whom God was previously incarnate.

He cannot be incarnated in a person who is not thoroughly prepared. This preparation takes years, and only one who has passed all the tests of both his teacher and God can be considered fit for God to be incarnated in him.

Petros passed all the tests from his teacher and from God, and He decided to incarnate in him. If the earth were not in danger from Satan, God would have been incarnate in this person without anyone knowing it. But because the earth is in danger from Satan, He decided to make this incarnation known, as He did when He incarnated in Christ.

A few of the people God has incarnated include Moses, to whom God dictated the Ten Commandments. King Nebuchadnezzar. King Solomon (the book of Solomon was not written by King Solomon but by some sorcerers who wanted to exploit King Solomon's name). He was also incarnated in Plato. The books Plato wrote were written with God's help, but not at his dictation. Another person in whom God was incarnate was Christ's father, Joseph.

When God became incarnate in Christ, he made his First Coming and performed many miracles. He also dictated to him Our Father, the Sermon on the Mount, and the words he said when he gave his disciples the bread and the wine.

He was also incarnate in Petros' teacher, as mentioned above, and now in Petros. These are just a few of the people he has incarnated. God loves all the people in whom He has incarnated.

All of God's incarnations have been important, but God's incarnation in Petros is more important because God decided to make his Second Coming.

God, like every human being, has the need to work; through work he feels fulfillment and satisfaction. He wants to help people and in a direct way, so he incarnates in people who wish to do the same thing. If it weren't for these individuals, God would feel lonely and frustrated. He never allows the incarnation of one person in another person. It can only allow this in exceptional circumstances.

Furthermore, he wants to be useful to people, just as each person wishes to be useful to his fellow human beings. That is why he gets angry when he sees people who are his creation and whom he loves being oppressed, wronged, or made to do witchcraft on them.

God does not want people to oppress, wrong, or cast spells on other people. When people do that, it feels like any father would feel if he saw his child being wronged, oppressed, or doing sorceries on him.

He doesn't want people to wrong, oppress, or cast spells on other people. When people do this, it is as if they are doing it to God himself.

He wants all people to be able to see him as their father because he is their father. God does not want people to think that their natural father is their real father because he is not.

Their real father is God. The natural father of every child has created his child, but with God's help. The mother of each child has also created her child, but with God's help. He is both the father and mother of every child. He has created both the father and mother of every child, so he can be both the father and mother of every child.

God does not want people to think that because God is a man, a man is superior to a woman. God wants men and women to be equal.

He does not want people to think that God is a misogynist. He loves women as well as men.

God doesn't want people to think that he is racist. He loves all races because he made them himself.

He doesn't want people to think that He is a dictator because God loves freedom and wants all people to be free to do whatever they want as long as they don't restrict other people's freedom.

People need to understand that paradise on earth could not become a reality if God allowed people to continue to wrong, oppress, and cast spells on other people.

He does not want people to work like slaves. He wants work to be a source of joy for people. Furthermore, he will punish people who wrong, oppress, or cast spells on other people, and their punishment will be as if they had tried to wrong, oppress, or cast spells on God himself.

He does not want people to wrong, oppress, or make sorceries, just as they would not want other people to do these evil things to them.

God, who has so much power, never wants to wrong or oppress people. And Satan, who has no power at all, wants to wrong, oppress, and make sorceries on other people; he wants to dominate them, and his goal is to prevail over the whole earth.

He will never allow Satan to do that. If Satan were to succeed in dominating the entire earth, God would cause such great natural disasters that all humans would die. Except for a very few who would live to begin a new cycle of life again, as He has already mentioned.

In fact, Satan's struggle to dominate the entire earth is already lost for him because even if he succeeded in dominating the entire earth, God would destroy it to begin a new cycle of life on earth.

He is responsible for what happens on earth. If God sees that Satan is about to dominate the entire earth, then He will destroy it.

The person who is writing this book with God's dictation is ready to give even his life so that Satan will not prevail on earth. God loves him and will protect him in every way.

Another subject God wants to speak about is my teacher's death. My teacher was sick in his heart, but he would have lived longer if God had not wanted to make his Second Coming. He let St. Joseph Buck Phong's health deteriorate with my teacher's consent.

God decided this when he saw that he could incarnate in Petros. St. Joseph Buck Phong and God decided that in order for God to incarnate in Petros, St. Joseph Buck Phong first had to incarnate in Petros to help him because Satan was doing many sorceries to him.

The nearly modern ark

God was about to destroy the entire world because Satan, together with organized crime, was about to dominate Greece and the entire world. God only changed his decision when he saw that he could incarnate in Petros.

My teacher died, and with his death, he saved the entire world. God had instructed my teacher in 2003 to gather as many animals as he could at his home in Keratea, Greece.

My teacher's house would become the modern ark. My teacher had gathered many animals that were always in pairs. When people asked my teacher what he would do with all these animals, he would say, "I want to make an ark." But no man, including myself, had realized God's actual plan.

My teacher would not die so quickly to pass on his knowledge and guide the surviving individuals to the new cycle of life on earth.

God wishes to tell people that, thanks to these two people, his reign on earth has begun to be realized. Good people should not be afraid; only those who wrong, oppress, or cast spells on other people should be afraid and repent. If they do not repent, God's punishment will be immediate and harsh.

The Father, the Son, and the Holy Spirit

Through this book, he wants people to know God better. Furthermore, he wants people to know better who the Father, the Son, and the Holy Spirit are.

God is the father of all people because He created them. The Son is all people throughout the earth. The Holy Spirit is the wisdom and knowledge of God.

He wants all people throughout the earth to know God, i.e., their Father, better. He also wants them to know more about their brothers and sisters, who are all people all over the earth. Likewise, he wants them to know more about the Holy Spirit, who is the wisdom and knowledge of God.

God loves all people all over the earth because they are his children. Without children, there can be no father either. God wants all people all over the earth to consider him their Father, to ask in prayer what they need and what they want, and God the Father will give it to them. There is no wish that God the Father cannot fulfill as long as it does not restrict the freedom of his other children. This book that God gave to men is his wisdom and his truth, i.e., it is the Holy Spirit. This book is the gospel of God because God himself has dictated it. He wants all people to love and believe in him. He would not make all these promises that he makes to people if he could not keep them.

Nor would he ask people to ask him for whatever proof they want that this book is from the true God. He loves this book and wants people all over the earth to love it, too.

How God delivered the Israelites

In this book, God wants to tell the true story of how He helped the Israelites be delivered from the slavery of the ancient Egyptians mentioned in the Old Testament. Moses was a slave, along with the rest of the Israelites. The ancient Egyptians were tough on the Israelites. One day, an Egyptian guard began beating Moses to make him work faster. Moses, in his anger, hit and killed this guard. After this, Moses fled in secret because, if he were caught, he would be killed.

God met Moses in the desert, where he lived alone. God forgave Moses for what he had done and prepared him to become incarnate in him. After Moses went through all of God's trials, God became incarnate in him. After a period of about ten years, Moses went back to the Egyptian camp to free his countrymen, as God had promised him.

God, who was incarnate in Moses, began to perform miracles that only the Israelites could see in order for the Israelites to believe in the power of God. At the same time, he was punishing the Egyptians.

The Israelites believed in God and decided to follow him on the journey to freedom. This journey lasted about five years.

During this journey, the Israelites ate the celery root, as God had advised them to do.

That is why they took several of these roots with them. This root needs very little water to grow, so they were able to grow and eat it during their journey in the desert. They also drank water from a container that, with God's help, was filled with water from the sun.

The Red Sea was not opened for the Israelites to cross, but with God's help, they walked on it to cross over to the other side.

God, in this case, did the same miracle that He did with Christ when He walked on water. God helped the Israelites so much because He had compassion for them and because the Israelites believed in God.

The difference between hate and anger

We should never judge other people, even Satan. Satan judges people, and the ones who do not meet his criteria, he makes sorceries on them and sometimes enslaves both their souls and immaterial bodies when they die.

God does not want us to judge people. He wants us to pray to God and ask for his help if a person has wronged us in any way. God will help us and also punish the person who has wronged us if he sees we are really right.

God does not want us to have hatred for anyone. We can be angry with a person who has wronged us, oppressed us, or done witchcraft to us, but not hate him. Hate makes us weaker and more vulnerable to Satan's attacks. Anyone who hates loses their strength, their ability to think clearly, and their connection to God.

The difference between hatred and anger is enormous. Someone who hates cannot forgive a person; someone who is angry can forgive.

Someone who hates cannot love, while someone who is angry can love.

Furthermore, someone who hates cannot enjoy life; someone who is angry can.

One who hates cannot have contact with God, but one who is angry can.

God does not want people to have hate; hate is from Satan. When we hate, we are with Satan. Satan wants people to have a hatred for other people because then he knows he can do whatever he wants to them. God doesn't want people to have hatred because then he can't help them. Only when we have love can God help us, and when we hate, we cannot have love.

The perfect God

God is perfect. Man is God's creation, and He wants all His creations to be perfect. Man can achieve this through his union with God.

The way man can achieve this is through prayer. Prayer is the Alpha and Omega of our union with God. God wants all men to be united with Him, all men to be perfect.

For a person to be perfect, i.e., united with God, he must be good and righteous and not do sorceries; he must pray to God daily; he must follow his commandments described in this book.

He must also be humble and ready to help his fellow man. He must have love in him, and he must have forgiveness. Furthermore, he must love children, he must have consideration for others, he must have truth, he must have justice, and he must have all these things together to be able to be perfect.

God doesn't want people to have all these by oppressing themselves; He wants all these to come out of them spontaneously because they will know that if they have all these, it will be in their best interest.

God helps people who have all this. The ways in which God helps people who have all these things are by giving them strength, love, inner peace, and a clear mind.

He also helps them by giving them what they ask Him for in their prayer and what He judges they need. He doesn't want people to pray all day to achieve all this. A few minutes each morning before we set out for work is enough.

If a person has all the things we have described, then they have a perfect balance. Balance is the alpha and omega of achieving our union with God. Righteousness is necessary to have balance, as is love. God wants all people to have justice, love, and balance because then He can help them more.

Satan's "house"

God does not want people to go to "Satan's house." When people go to Satan's "house," then Satan can do whatever he wants to them. Satan's "house" is the casinos, live sex shows, and brothels. When we go to these establishments, Satan, i.e., the sorcerers and witches, can do whatever they want to us.

He doesn't want people to gamble, watch live sex shows, or pay to have sex. When we do these things, we are with Satan. Paid sex is humiliating for the woman doing it and for the man. This sex is from Satan because there is no love in it.

When we watch a live sex show, Satan can do many sorceries on us; one of the most serious sorceries is with our love life. When we gamble, Satan can do many sorceries with our money.

He also does not want us to serve Satan. People serve Satan when they wear the most expensive clothing, or drive outrageously expensive cars, or have extravagantly expensive houses or items of exceptionally high value. When we have these things, it means we are interested in what we will show on the outside and not what we have on the inside.

God doesn't want people to be interested only in the outside. He wants them to be interested in their soul. If a person only cares about the image they present to the outside world, they lose their power, and Satan can more easily hurt them. God wants us to be more interested in the inside, namely our soul.

Another thing he doesn't want is for us to take money from Satan. When we take money from Satan, he can take our soul.

We get money from Satan when we lie for profit; we get money from Satan when we deceive other people; and we get money from Satan when we oppress or wrong other people.

He doesn't want us to do these bad things. When we do these bad things, then we are with Satan.

The laws of God

God wants to have contact with people; He wishes to help them and in a direct way. By helping people directly, he feels satisfaction, fulfillment, and joy.

God's job is to help all people all over the world, and he does this through the laws he has made and the interpretation of those laws that he establishes.

This is what he is doing, and through this book, what he writes will be the laws that will apply from now on. He is careful about every phrase that he writes in this book. He wants this book to be His gospel.

Anyone who breaks these laws will get the punishment they deserve, depending on how serious their offense is. God doesn't have to do anything to accomplish all of this. It all happens automatically because of the laws that he has made.

God knows everything that happens in the world. He doesn't need to see it on TV or hear it on the radio. He knows what people do overtly and what they do covertly, i.e., by sorceries. That is why we sometimes see some people being punished by God without having done anything overtly, but God also knows what these people do secretly.

When God punishes a country or a group of people, some innocent people suffer or are killed. He gets mournful and helps these people overcome their problems, or he sends them to paradise if they die.

God is not evil to punish people for no reason. When he punishes some people or a country, it is because he cannot do otherwise. If he let these people continue their work, then they would enslave the souls and bodies of all the people in this country.

It is better for a man to die and go to paradise, namely, to be born again on earth, than for Satan to enslave that man's soul and immaterial body. When Satan enslaves a person's soul and body, it is not at all pleasant for the person who has been enslaved. Satan can torture that person day and night to take all the power from that person and use it as he wants.

That is why God will never let Satan enslave the souls and bodies of people. All the sorcerers who have died will go to hell, and so will all those who die from now on.

Satan will not dominate the earth, nor will injustice or oppression. God will bring paradise to earth. Paradise can only come if Satan is defeated. Satan can be defeated if people believe in this book. Injustice, oppression, and witchcraft will stop. Justice, joy, and love will prevail on earth.

He wants to help people all over the world. God's help will be just according to the degree to which people believe in this book. Because God does not want to help people if they do not deserve it.

If He helped people without them deserving it, then people would not know how to improve themselves. If people in some part of the earth or on a continent don't believe this book, then God will not bring paradise to that part of the earth until people believe there too.

He will do this not because He is evil, but because He wants all people to have justice, love, and balance. If people have paradise without these three basic ingredients, then paradise will be fake. God doesn't want a fake paradise. He wants the real one. The real paradise has justice, love, and balance; it has a right to self-expression; and it has truth.

Truth is something that God loves; without truth, there is no paradise. He wishes all people to have truth. Without truth, there can be no justice, no love, and no balance. Balance wants truth. God would not have decided to write this book if he had not wanted to tell the truth. He wants to tell the truth so that his Second Coming will have nothing that is not truth.

He also wanted to tell the truth at his First Coming by dictating many books to Christ, but he didn't have time because Satan killed Christ before he could write those books. This time, he has written this book, which consists of six shorter books. He will do many miracles, as He did with Christ, so that people will believe this book.

He will give people whatever proof they ask for. But he does not want people to blame this book before they ask God for proof. If people believe in this book and obey the basic laws, then God will give them everything they need to be happy.

Hell, Purgatory, and Paradise

Through this book, he wants to give a gift to all people on earth. God's gift is for people to know where hell is. Hell is on the moon. The moon is a place with no life at all. It is too hot during the day and too cold at night. The souls, along with the immaterial bodies that are there, get too hot during the day and too cold at night.

There are no friends because each soul is isolated from the other souls. There are big birds that sting these people and dogs that bite them. All these are intangible, and no one can see them, even with the most advanced equipment.

God doesn't tell people all this to scare them; he wants them to know the truth. Sorcerers and witches have so far avoided hell by performing sorceries before their deaths, and so they thought hell did not exist.

Hell, though, does exist, and all sorcerers and witches will go there after their death unless they repent. God has so far allowed sorcerers and witches to avoid hell so that people could see the difference between good and evil, but from now on, he will not allow this.

He will never allow people who are on the moon to leave from there because if they do, the earth will be in danger. The people there are so evil that if they left, they would enslave the whole earth. God wants to abolish hell, but that will happen after thousands of years. God would like to abolish purgatory too, but that will happen after thousands of years.

He wants all people to go to paradise, i.e., to return to earth to live a new life. Paradise is the earth; here are the climatic conditions for people to live and be happy.

Through this book, he wants to give another great gift to people; he wishes to reveal to them where purgatory is. Purgatory is on Saturn. On Saturn, people don't get cold or hot like on the moon. The difference between Saturn and the moon is enormous.

On the moon, souls stay there forever. On Saturn, they return to Earth after five to ten years. Communication between people is not possible on the moon, but it is possible on Saturn. On the moon, it is freezing at night and too hot during the day. On Saturn, the climatic conditions are generally much better. On the moon there is no mercy for people; on Saturn there is.

Paradise is the earth. He wants to help people live in paradise on earth. He wishes to help them live with justice, love, and balance. If the earth acquires justice, love, and balance, then it will have paradise just like the other two planets inhabited by people have.

God will give the people on earth all the knowledge that He has given to the people living on the other two planets. He will help them overcome all problems as long as people do not violate God's laws of justice, love, and balance.

How to cure mental traumas

God wants to give people a way to be able to cure the mental traumas of the past. This can be done with God's help. The person who has suffered mental trauma should pray to God and ask for his help in this matter. God will help that person if he is good and righteous and does not do sorceries.

The way God will help this person is through a dream that he will send him. People will know when they will have overcome a mental trauma when they have no hatred for the person who has hurt them and no anger, either. They will trust God to do justice for what has been done to them and will not want to retaliate for the harm.

The natural disasters

God wants to bring paradise to earth. The earth is His creation, and so is man, and He loves them very much. If he had not loved the earth, he would have destroyed it. He loves the earth because it is perfect, like all his creations. The earth was made by God to be perfect.

Humans are destroying the earth with nuclear testing, chemical fertilizers, and sorceries. Nuclear testing is destroying the earth because it produces radioactivity that is harmful to the environment and humans. Chemical fertilizers destroy the soil and water, and sorceries force God to create natural disasters to fight Satan.

If God had not made these natural disasters, Satan would have dominated the earth a long time ago. God is forced to make earthquakes, floods, droughts, and tornadoes to fight Satan, but Satan does not stop. He will punish Satan harshly if he doesn't stop doing sorceries and destroying the lives of thousands of people.

When God tries to punish some people for the bad things they do, other areas of the earth may suffer a natural disaster. This is because all parts of the earth are connected and interact with each other.

He always gets sorrowful when he sees innocent people suffer from natural disasters, but he cannot let bad people destroy the earth. This is another reason He wants to bring paradise to earth as soon as possible, so that all these natural disasters will stop.

Consideration for others

For there to be justice, love, and balance, there must be consideration for others. Consideration for others is something that God loves. Consideration for others is a component of paradise.

Paradise wants people with consideration for others to work while having all the necessities for their survival. Having all the necessities but wanting a better quality of life. To have a better quality of life but want the same for their fellow man.

God loves people who have consideration for others because he knows these people can go to paradise, i.e., be born again on earth, without first having to go through purgatory. When a person is born again on earth without first having to go through purgatory, God gives him or her privileges.

The privileges that he gives to these individuals are many. One privilege is that he chooses a good family to send them to. Another privilege is that they have God's guidance in their lives. Another privilege is that he gives them more wisdom.

These privileges that He gives to these individuals can be lost if they are not good and righteous or if they practice witchcraft. Or they may increase them if they are good people.

The environment

The environment must be protected. People need to respect the environment and not pollute it with chemical or nuclear waste. Every country must respect the environment and do everything possible to protect it. God will punish countries that do not respect the environment, and the same will happen to people or companies that do not respect the environment.

It will give knowledge to help people overcome problems related to the environment. One of these pieces of knowledge is the invention that will enable all people on earth to be provided free electricity with the force of gravity.

Another knowledge that God will give to people is that they will be able to fly with the special shell and go to any place on earth they want with the power of magnetic attraction. He will make this invention soon. This device will become a reality on earth, and all people will be able to use it.

Another knowledge that God wants to give people is the ability to clean up an area that has been contaminated by nuclear energy after a nuclear accident, with efficiency and with very little money. The way we can do this is to wet that area with water and then pour salt on top of it. The proportion of salt should be the same as the salt we would put in our food. We leave this salt for ten days and then rinse with water. This method can be repeated until the area is completely clean.

Another knowledge that God wants to give is to have everywhere on the whole earth an ideal climate. He can accomplish this by making a second sun for the earth.

This second sun will provide light but also dewiness when needed. In this way, He will bring sunshine everywhere on the entire earth during the day. All the ice will melt on earth without an inch of it disappearing. He will keep the temperature of the earth at about 25 degrees Celsius.

This temperature is ideal for humans. Nature will continue to function as it does now. The trees will blossom and shed their leaves at the right time. The big forest fires will stop because there will not be very high temperatures and strong winds. God wants to bring paradise to earth, and paradise without an ideal climate cannot exist.

Wants to help people in other ways, too. He wishes to give them all the knowledge that he himself has about subjects such as mathematics and the study of the universe.

From the money saved from this knowledge, he wants it to be used to assist the people who need it most. Never should this knowledge be used for military purposes. God wants this knowledge to be used with justice, love, and balance.

Another issue he wants to talk about is the exploitation of the earth. The earth is made by God in such a way that it can give us everything, as long as we do not destroy it with pesticides and chemical or nuclear waste. People should use natural fertilizers to cultivate the earth.

GOD AND CHRIST: THE TRUE STORY OF CHRIST

God decided to tell people the story of Christ. Christ was born in a city that was by the sea, near Ashkelon, Israel. God, after all these years, does not remember the name of this city, nor do Holy Mary or Christ. There was the town where he lived with his mother and father for the whole of his life.

God was incarnate in his father when Christ was born. Christ was a normal child who liked to play with other children; he also liked school. Christ went up to the sixth grade. Back then, children didn't need to go longer to school; only the wealthy children continued school.

Jesus' father was healing people with massage and various herbs. God was incarnate in Jesus' father and helped him in the treatments he did. Little Jesus helped his dad from a very young age. His mother, Holy Mary, helped the family by knitting socks and sweaters. Jesus had a younger sister. Christ's sister's name was Mary.

God loved Christ very much and helped him from a young age. Christ, with God's help, advanced a lot and became ready for God to be incarnated in him. When Christ's father could no longer work because he was too old, he became incarnate in Christ. Christ was always obedient to God, never displeased him, and always did his will.

Christ began performing miracles with God's help at twenty-three, two years after God became incarnate in him. Jesus performed many miracles with God's help. He healed blind people, raised Lazarus, healed paralytic people, pulled demons out of people, fed many people with the little food he had, walked on water, and healed people with serious mental illnesses.

People loved and admired him. But there were some people who did not like the miracles that Christ performed. These people were the sorcerers and witches.

The church was very cautious about the miracles that Christ performed because they did not know that only God could perform miracles and never Satan.

Christ's life went on with no problems; he did miracles and practiced fishing for a living. God was helping Christ catch many fish, so he did not have to work as a healer.

Immediately, Christ had many disciples and taught them what God dictated to him. Among his disciples, he singled out seven and taught only them. The disciples who were with Christ were Peter, Matthew, John, Mark, Paul, James, and Timothy.

All of his disciples practiced the profession of fisherman. Jesus often went to Jerusalem and, from there, to other nearby cities with his disciples to perform miracles. Three years after he began the miracles, he was falsely accused by Satan and crucified.

After Christ's death, God was forced to go to Asia, where he stayed several years close to a healer, prepared him, and incarnated in him.

God has been incarnated in various people since the beginning of the creation of the world. First, because He wants to experience all the difficulties faced by ordinary people; second, to help people and in a direct way; and third, because if He did not incarnate in a person, He would feel lonely and disappointed.

He always wishes to help people, and directly, because God does not have to do anything to help people all over the world. It is all done automatically by the laws he has made himself.

Only in exceptional cases does he come out of the body of the person who has incarnated to help or punish some people when his laws are not sufficient for a particular case.

God is love, so He likes to love people and to be loved. He wants to have all the love in the world; that's why he helps them so much. He wants not to take the energy from people; he wishes to give them his energy; he does not wish to take the love of the people; he wishes to give them his love; he wants not to have servants; he wants to serve.

God wants people to love him so he can help them. He wants them to respect him so he can respect them as well. He wants them to pray to him so that he can help them.

All of God's incarnations were secret, except Christ's and now Petros'. God made his incarnation in Christ known to teach people how to treat their fellow man and, by his incarnation in Petros, to bring paradise to earth.

God wanted to do even more miracles with Christ and teach people even more things, but Satan did not let him complete his work.

Satan did not defeat God. God restored the name of Jesus and made a new religion, Christianity. He wants to tell people that Satan will not stop him a second time and that he will bring the paradise to earth that he has promised them. He will bring paradise to earth; otherwise, Satan would bring hell to earth.

God wants justice, love, and balance. Balance is a key component of paradise. In order for balance to exist, there must be justice and love. He does not want justice for the few but for all people, and the same is true for love.

Justice has two sides: the justice of the individual and the justice of society. The justice of society depends on the justice of the individual, and vice versa.

Love also has two sides: the love of the individual and the love of society. The love of society depends on the love of the individual, and vice versa.

Balance also has two sides: the balance of the individual and the balance of society. The balance of society depends on the balance of the individual, and vice versa.

The Crucifixion of Christ

God wants all people to learn the story of Christ so that they will not repeat the same mistakes. If people repeat the same mistakes, then God will destroy the whole earth. Christ died because he was falsely accused.

Peter, who was a disciple of Christ, went to buy a camel, and the camel salesman sold him an older camel. Peter, when he noticed that the camel that had been sold to him was old, went back to the camel owner and asked him to give him another camel. The Camel salesman refused, and Peter, in his anger, called him names. Satan then performed many sorceries on the camel owner, and everyone thought Jesus had done the sorceries because he was Peter's teacher.

Christ learned that he had been accused of the sorceries that the sorcerers and witches had done to the camel owner and that the next morning they would come to arrest him. The reason they didn't come to arrest him that day is because it was the Sabbath. Jesus wanted to prove that he was innocent, but no one believed him.

God said to Jesus not to be afraid and that He would protect him. He asked him to inform his disciples and to meet at John's house, where he would tell him what to do.

When Christ met with his disciples, they embraced and wept. God asked Christ to prepare the bread and wine and to say the words that Christ said as he gave the bread and wine to his disciples. He did as God told him, and immediately afterward, they all left and went to their homes.

God wanted to protect Christ, but people would think that Christ was the incarnation of Satan and would accuse him doubly. God felt profound sorrow for Christ's death but also anger at the people who accused him unjustly.

Christ was examined by a small group of people, and they decided on his crucifixion. Immediately after the decision, they took Christ to crucify him.

Christ never went through a proper court of law. His examination was brief and biased. Crucifixion was the cruelest form of punishment and was only meant for people who had killed other people.

Christ was forced to carry his cross to the place of martyrdom; on the way, they were whipping him, swearing at him, and spitting on him. They put a crown of wire on his head, which had sharp ends to pierce his head; they dressed him in an orange robe; and they put a sign on him that read "Jesus the King." They gave him vinegar to drink, and they also put it on the wounds he had on his back and head. His feet were bare and full of blood from the sharp stones.

When Christ arrived at the place of martyrdom, they laid him on the cross, where nails had been placed to pierce his back as well. Put nails all the way along his arms up to his shoulders. They did the same on the legs; they put many nails up to the thighs. Then they broke his teeth by giving him vinegar with a sponge tied to a stick. When they lifted the cross, they put vinegar on his wounds, swearing at him and beating him with a big stick so that he would die.

Jesus never asked God to forgive the people who did this because he was certain that God would punish them. God punished harshly all those who were responsible for what they did to him.

Christ became a saint after his death, and he has been united with God until now to help him in his work. God wants to tell people not to repeat the same mistake they made with Christ because, first, He will not let them, and second, He will punish them hard.

God wishes to tell people that this time it will not be like it was with Christ, when life went on as normal after his death. This time, he will destroy the entire world because he cannot bring paradise to earth by himself.

He also wants to inform people that paradise is very close, as is the destruction of the earth. If people believe this book, paradise will be here; if they reject it, ignoring God's proofs, then Satan will prevail on earth. If Satan prevails on earth, it will force God to destroy the whole earth. God does not want to destroy the entire earth. He wants to save it.

Satan is ready to impose hell on earth, and, if it were not for God, he would have already succeeded. He will never let Satan impose hell on earth. God intends to bring paradise to earth, while Satan intends to bring hell. Satan would like to make life on earth a hell. He wants to enslave the entire planet and the souls and bodies of people when they die so that he can have more power.

God wants peace, love, and justice. Satan wants injustice, hatred, and greed and has the need to control everyone and everything. Satan wants to control everything because he wants to dominate people and do whatever he wants to them. God wants people to be free to do whatever they want, as long as they do not restrict the freedom of other people.

Satan wants to have power; God wants love; God wishes to have justice; Satan wants to have justice on his side; Satan wants sorceries; God wants creation. God wishes to tell people they should not trust Satan because Satan, when he no longer needs them, will throw them away. God will always be with them.

He wants to tell people they should detest Satan and love God. God wishes to have peace; Satan wants war. God wants justice; Satan wants justice in his small pocket. God wants love; Satan wants a fuss.

Satan wants justice in his small pocket so that he can blackmail and kill people with his sorceries without anyone being able to do anything to him. He wants a fuss so he can fool people, and he wants hate so he can control people.

God wants to have love so that he can help people. He wishes to have justice so that he can have power, and he wishes to have peace so that he can have happiness.

Satan wants to have peace by killing all who disobey him. He wants to have justice on his side, and he wants to have love by force.

God wishes to have all; Satan has nothing. God has all because he is all. Satan has nothing because he demands them all. God has all; Satan has nothing. God has them all because He made them all. Satan has nothing because he steals them all.

Satan wants to dominate the earth. God wants to save it. Satan wants to have the upper hand. God has a heavy hand. God has a heavy hand for those who oppress, wrong, or make sorceries. The hand of God will be even heavier on the mobsters and sorcerers. Mafiosi and sorcerers have been warned by God, but they ignore him and continue their work. God will send all sorcerers and all mafiosi to hell.

God sends only the worst people to hell. The ones who consciously and repeatedly hurt other people. God is righteous if these people want to enslave the whole earth. And if, despite God's warnings, they do not repent, then the punishment they deserve is hell.

God wants justice. He will never give a punishment to a man who does not deserve it. He wants peace, and he will never give a punishment to a man who does not deserve it. Furthermore, he wants love and will never give a punishment to a man who does not deserve it.

He wants to tell people the story of Christ. Christ was not God. Christ never said, I am God. What he said is that "I and my father are one." That is true, and that is a phrase that Petros and Petros' teacher, St. Joseph Buck Phong can say.

Saint Joseph Buck Phong never said to anyone that God was incarnate in him. So did Petros; for three years, he had said nothing to anyone about God's incarnation in him, and he would not have ever said it if God had not revealed it through this book.

God is the Father, not only of Christ but of all men throughout the earth. He is the father of all men because He has created them. He wants all people to call him their father and to feel that way because that is who he is. After all, that is what people say in "Our Father," which is not a mere figure of speech but is the truth.

The Second Coming of God

God decided to make His Second Coming because He saw the earth was in danger from Satan. If the earth was not in danger from Satan, God would not have made His Second Coming. God wants to tell people that Petros is one with God, and God is one with Petros. Christ was one with God, and God was one with Christ. Christ never said he was God. If Christ were the God, he would have said it.

People made up the story of Christ according to what they knew. That is why God allowed so many years for people to think that Christ is God. God knows people did this out of love for Christ, so He allowed it. Christ was born in a town near Ashkelon, where his parents lived. He grew up there and was crucified there.

God restored the name of Christ and made a new religion, Christianity. Without God's help, Christ would have been unknown. God loved Christ very much; Christ always did God's will. He never displeased God, and he never wanted people to think that he was God.

If Christ wanted people to think He was God, He would have said so. Christ was always obedient to God; he never did or said anything that was not from God.

God wants to thank Christ for his help. Without Christ, people would not know about miracles, neither Our Father's prayer nor Holy Communion. God gave these three things to people, thanks to Christ. He loves Christ, and he will never forget how much he offered to people.

Jesus' father did not go to stand by his son when he was being crucified and said a bad word about his son, so God did not make him a saint.

After many years, God decided to have as his second name the name St. Joseph so that people would have a picture of God in their minds about God. When people would pray to St. Joseph, they would actually pray to God.

Christ's father, Joseph, was always obedient to God and never displeased him. God did not punish Joseph for not standing by his son, but neither could he make him a saint. His mother, Holy Mary, was always close to him, so God made her a saint. Peter and the other disciples of Christ did not continue his work because God did not incarnate in any of them.

Pilate did not exist; Israel had been liberated then with God's help. God would never have made His First Coming in a country that was under occupation. A group of people condemned Christ.

Christ never appeared to any of his disciples after his death. He never said he would rise in three days. What he said was that after his death, God would put him on his right side, as he did.

God made Christ a saint and gave him the ability to help any man who would pray to him. Christ never said to tear down the walls of Jerusalem and rebuild them in three days. He never said that Peter would be with him after his death because only God decides that. God sent Peter to purgatory for verbally abusing the camel salesman, even though he knew he had to be careful.

God decided to kill all those who were responsible for Jesus' death and crucifixion. He also sent to hell the sorcerers who had harmed him and one of the group who condemned Jesus for collaborating with the sorcerers. He punished the soldiers who crucified him because they were especially cruel to him. He decided to punish the people who spat on him and insulted him without him having done anything to them.

He punished the people who, after Christ's death, treated Holy Mary badly. He punished the people who wanted Christ's death and decided to punish the people who lied so that Christ would be condemned. God did not leave anyone unpunished. His punishment was just according to the evil that each person did.

God wants to tell people not to repeat the same mistake. Christ was unjustly crucified because there was no justice, love, and balance. God wishes to tell people that if they repeat the same mistake, then he will destroy the whole earth. God wishes to bring paradise to earth. Petros helps God bring paradise to earth.

Petros would already be dead if he didn't have God's protection. God protects Petros and punishes those who try to harm him. He punishes those who try to harm him according to the severity of the harm they tried to do to him. God knows all those who attempt to harm him, and He punishes them. If it were not for Petros, God would have had to destroy the entire world.

Petros always does God's will, has never displeased Him, and has never broken the promises he has made to God. God loves him and wants to give him a present. His present to Petros is that Petros may have God's blessing. God's blessing is a present that he gives to especially good people when they die. Petros has not died, but he is risking his life daily because he wrote this book with God's dictation.

God loves him and wants to give Petros one more present. Petros will be able to have the blessing of the people. When a man has the blessing of men, he is immortal. God gives this present only to those who have given much to humanity. Immortal does not mean that he will never die, but that his name will be immortal throughout the ages.

God wants to give Petros another present. God's present to Petros is that Petros may have the blessing of the church. The church is God's. God decides which people can have God's blessing. Every time the church has a mass, Petros will also be blessed.

God also wishes to thank Petros' teacher, St. Joseph Buck Phong. Petros' teacher gave his life so that Satan would not prevail on earth. He loves him and wants to give him a present. God's present to St. Joseph Buck Phong is that he may have the blessing of God, of the people, and of the church. God is just; if there was no St. Joseph Buck Phong, there would be no Petros. Petros exists because God exists. If God did not protect Petros, Petros would not exist.

God protects Petros. One way is by taking out the sorceries that Satan does to him; another way is by punishing the people who try to hurt him; one more way is by having all the powers guarding and God Himself to protect him; yet another way is by having Petros at God's table; still another way is by advising Petros what to do in every situation; and yet another way is by this book.

These ways are from God. Petros does not want to hurt anyone. God, however, does. He wants to punish people who try to hurt Petros.

God will punish all the mafiosi and all the sorcerers who attempt to harm Petros. The mafiosi and sorcerers ignore the warnings from God and continue their work. God would like to warn them one more time and tell them that if they do not repent, they will die and go to hell. He also wants to warn all those who help them so they can take money from them.

God would also like to warn the church not to make the same mistakes again. Not to "crucify Christ again" in Christ's name. The church can ask for whatever proof it wants that this book is from God. If the church ignores this book or blames it without first asking for proof from God, then God will punish all those responsible. God wants the church to be his ally, not across from him.

God also wants to tell people that Petros is one with God, just as Christ was. Christ was falsely accused and crucified, which is why God protects Petros so well. God has Petros at his table. This means that Petros and God eat together. Petros eats, and God eats with him. God loves Petros so much for one more reason. When Petros hurts, God hurts too. Another reason God loves Petros so much is because Petros has the same body as God. God's body is immaterial, and when He is incarnated in a person, then that person's body becomes God's body as well.

The saints who are united with God help him in his work. One way is by helping people pray to the saints so that God can help them. Another way is by communicating with some people to help them, and another way is by always doing His will.

God wants to thank all the saints for their help. Petros can communicate with Christ, the Holy Mary, Pope John Paul II, and, of course, his teacher, St. Joseph Buck Phong.

How Satan works

God wants all people to have justice and balance, and when a person has balance, then he has justice and love. Love is necessary for God to help a person. Satan does sorceries to take love away from people because then he knows he can hurt them more easily. The ways Satan takes love from people are many.

One way is by scaring them, another way is by making them angry, and another way is by making them hate other people. Another way is by making them not love their spouse; another way is by making their children not love them; and another way is by making their friends and acquaintances not love them.

All these ways are from Satan. Satan is cunning; he is doing his work in secret and without people knowing, but God knows what they are doing and will punish them. His punishment will be hell. God wants justice. If these people are destroying the lives of thousands of people, then the punishment they deserve is hell.

Satan will not defeat God. All sorcerers and witches will go to hell, and so will the members of this criminal organization. Its members swear to Satan. Satan helps them, and they help Satan. The sorcerers and witches have the help of other sorcerers who have died. The sorcerers who have died are nothing more than the demons.

God will expel the demons from all the earth. These demons are helping Satan very much. One way that demons help Satan is by getting into people's bodies to lead them to madness or death; another way is by going into people's homes to frighten them; another way is by watching what people do in their homes so that Satan can more easily make sorceries at them; and another way is by putting sorceries in people's homes.

Another way is by roaring, making loud bangs, or making various noises outside and sometimes inside people's houses to scare them.

God has so far allowed this for three reasons. First, because it was not a big threat; second, so that people would see the difference between good and evil; and third, because he had not made his Second Coming.

God wants justice, love, and balance. When a man has these, God will help him with any problem or task. He wants all people to be happy and free. Satan wants all people to be under his control. God wants all people to have everything; Satan wants all people to have nothing. God wants all people to have his blessing. When all people have his blessing, then they can have paradise.

A person will know they have God's blessing when God is with them. A person will know that God is with him when he feels God within him. God wants all people to feel God in them. God wants all people to feel God in them because God is in every person. The essence of God is in every person, even if that person is evil.

God wants all people to be in communication with the essence of God that is within them. People can achieve this if they have justice, love, and balance. God has only one body, which is immaterial, but his essence is within each person.

Paradise is God's blessing, and God wants all people to experience Paradise on earth. Paradise on earth is here, and people can live it if they have justice, love, and balance. Balance is something Satan hates. Satan wants all people to have no balance, i.e., to have no justice and love.

The ways Satan tries to make people lose balance are many. One way is through sorceries; another way is by making people think God does not exist; another way is by making people think that hell does not exist.

Another way that Satan makes people lose balance is by making sorceries so that they can't sleep well. Satan makes sorceries at people to keep them from sleeping, to make them tired, so he can then make easier sorceries at them.

Another way Satan makes people lose their balance is by sending them bad dreams. Another way is to make them think they are going to die; another way is to make them think they are sick; and another way is to make them think they have done something bad when they have done nothing.

Satan wants people to be afraid so he can do what he wants to them. God wants to tell people they should not be afraid of Satan; they should pray to God and ask for his help.

The church does not believe in this book yet, but when they see the miracles from God, they will believe that this book is from God. God loves the church. If it were not for the church, God would not have a place for people to worship Him and ask for His help, which He would gladly give to them. God wants to help the church become stronger. He wants all people all over the earth to believe in the church, in the power of God, and in his love for people.

God will not help any man who has not been baptized in the church as a Christian. He wants all people around the world to believe in this book, be baptized, and pray to God so that God can help them. God wants paradise to come to earth. If people don't believe in the church, God cannot bring paradise to earth.

God wants paradise to come to earth because He wants all people to be happy. He wants justice, love, and balance to prevail. He wants there to be peace throughout the earth. Furthermore, he wants there to be a perfect climate; he wants people not to have to work like slaves; he wants all people to have food, water, and shelter even when they are not working.

God wants to defeat Satan, but he needs the help of the people for that and also the help of the church. God wishes to defeat Satan so that he can bring paradise to earth. Paradise on earth can only come if Satan is defeated. Satan can be defeated if people believe in God.

This book is written by God to defeat Satan so that He can bring paradise to earth. God wants to bring paradise to earth, but people also must want paradise to come to earth.

People can ask for this in their prayer, telling Our Father. In Our Father, we say, "Thy kingdom come, Thy will be done on earth as it is in heaven." When the kingdom of

God has come on earth, paradise will also have come on earth, which is God's will.

Paradise can only exist on earth if there is justice, love, and balance. If there is justice, love, and balance, there will be safety not only among people but also among nations. Wars and various crimes will stop, and so will sorceries. God will stop making natural disasters because he won't have to anymore and will give people knowledge to overcome various problems. He will give them free food with the three containers, as God has described.

He will also make the shell with which people will fly and go to any part of the earth they want with no cost and in complete safety; he will make a house for any person who needs one; and he will make the whole earth fertile without there being any desert.

God will accomplish all this if people believe in this book. Otherwise, Satan, with the assistance of organized crime, will prevail on earth, as God has mentioned before.

If this happens, God will have no choice but to destroy the entire earth and start a new cycle of life on earth. God will have no choice because He cannot leave humans in the hands of Satan.

Paradise on earth can come quickly if people believe in God, his power, and his love for them. God wants to bring paradise to earth, which is why He wanted to give this book to people through Petros.

In finishing this book, God would like to write some more things about Christ. Christ, when he died, was only 26 years old. If he had not died, he would have married and had a family. Another thing Christ would have done if he had not died so soon would have been to write books that God would have dictated to him. God wanted to dictate many books to Christ so that people would believe and repent.

One reason God waited so long to make his Second Coming is for people to see that the miracles can only be done by God and never by Satan. Satan can do sorceries, but he can never do miracles. God will do many miracles for people to believe in this book.

***

The more people who read this book, the sooner God will bring paradise to earth.

If you liked this book and believe it is from God, help other people learn about it.

If you liked this book and believe it is from God, help other people learn about it.

About the Author

Petros Koumasonas was born and raised in Athens, Greece. He studied psychology and psychotherapy and practiced this profession for several years. He is married and has one child.

His teacher, Joseph Buck Phong, was sick from his heart, which is why God decided to incarnate in Petros. His teacher died in 2005, and God incarnated in him two years later. God dictated this book to him from July 2010 until January 2012.

God passed Petros through many trials before deciding to incarnate in him. Petros always does God's will and writes only what God dictates to him.

Website: https://www.secondcomingofgod.com

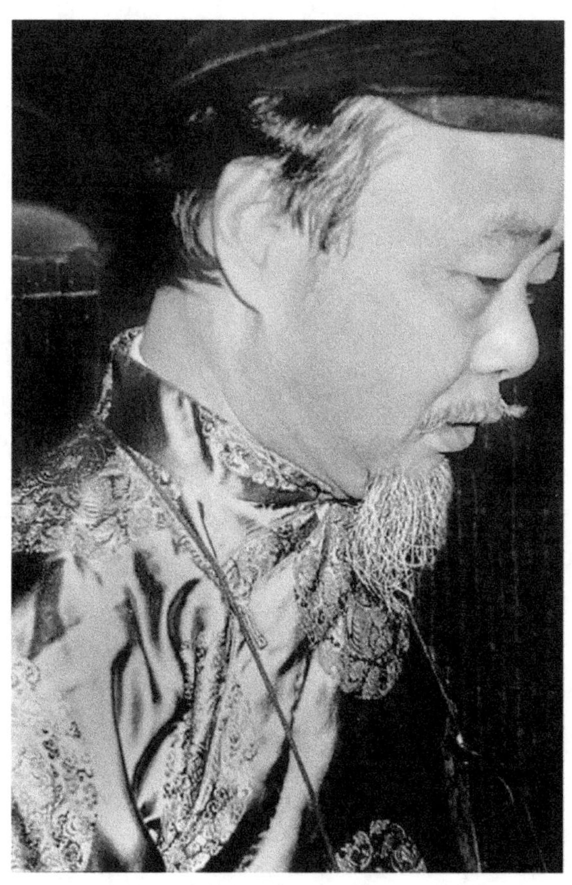

The teacher of Petros Saint Joseph Buck Phong
Born in Vietnam (1946-2005)